John
The treasure we all Seek,
lies deep within
the cave we fear to enter.

ISBN: 978-1-8381793-6-6

Dedication

To all those who woke up one morning and decided they wanted more. Be that more time, more money, more freedom.

I dedicate this, to all those who had a dream, and are in pursuit of making it a reality.

Table of Content

Testimonials

The book I wish I'd read 22 years ago. Jay is a great speaker a great coach and a great guy, very few people can aspire to all three.

Gerald Ratner
Former Chairman and CEO of Ratner's Jewellers

-

If you've got a business challenge, as you're scaling up, you're almost certain to find the answer you're looking for within ADDAZERO.

Jay has done some superb work pulling together everything you need to take your business to the next level. From marketing to sales to finance and building your team – Jay shares his deep wisdom. Get this book, read it, and accelerate your growth.

David Jenyns
Founder & CEO, SYSTEMology

-

A 'Must Read'. Intuitive, instructive, and incisive. Highly recommended.

Stephen Fletcher JP FRSA
Founder & Managing Director, The Leaders Club

I have known Jay Allen, both personally and professionally, for many years and I never cease to be impressed by his incisiveness in business, his generosity in sharing his wealth of knowledge and his 100% commitment to ethical business frameworks. This book is a testament to all three. It is sure to be a real go-to for any business owner who wants to grow, scale and, if they so choose, sell their business. Congratulations Jay, it's a winner.

Ralph Watson
Master Coach, Speaker, Master Trainer of NLP, and President – Association for Professional Coaching

-

This book serves as an A-Z Business bible, a step-by-step guide, relevant for anyone who runs a business, big or small. It contains vast amounts of helpful tips for all ranges of audience – beginner or seasoned business owner.

Lana Quigley
Principal, Prima Ultima

-

Jay has produced a great compass for anyone in business. This book gives you the direction to help you find your goal and fulfil your ambition with small nuggets of information that can be put into practice to help you along your entrepreneurial journey.

Bobby Singh
Managing Director – Mr Mobile UK

Acknowledgements

153 National Business Failures, more than 117,000 business owners who completed our Scaleup Scorecard. A team of dedicated Business Analysts that enabled the data of this book to be written.

My TrueNORTH and the clients old and new with whom remain living proof we eat, sleep and breath #ADDAZERO and remain committed to being of service to each one on their Scaleup journey.

The team of proof-readers, type setters, graphics etc, that have persevered with me, and turned my frantic ramblings and *good ideas* into something useable, user-friendly and for which we can all be exceptionally proud.

My darling wife, for the ongoing support, belief, encouragement, and devotion she continues to give, enabling me to forever strive to do more, be more, achieve more.

And, to you, the reader. For picking this book off the shelf - I offer thanks, and reassurance, the best is yet to come.

Preface

It's taken over 7 years of research, more than 2 years of implementation, reviewing, tweaking, amending, retesting before we even began to commit words to paper!

Even then, we've continually applied, learnt, listened to both the markets, and observed the trends and data to ensure **every word** is as up to date, relevant and necessary in today's business world!

My **strong** recommendation is that you **do not** either buy or read this book in isolation, as this is the **sequel** to my first Scaleup book: #ADDAZERO: The Ultimate Guide to Sustainable Scale (Establishing Basecamp). *Available by visiting www.addazero.co.uk/shop*

Only once a business has strong and tested foundations, should you even begin to apply the more advanced Scaleup strategies within this book. Without doing so, you could be at risk of becoming a future statistic on which we continue to base our research – Building a SCALE business on unstable or insecure foundations, is a far greater risk than now scaling at all!

Finally, **this is not intended as a <u>reading</u> book**. And whilst a few have read it from cover to cover. It is designed, more of a step-by-step guide on what, where, who, when and how to significantly and sustainable scale up both you and your business.

Disclaimer: Owning this book **will not** fix any of the problems you may currently face. Implementing the strategies, recommendations and teachings within this book has enabled more than 8000 Business owners (just like you) to #ADDAZERO to their personal disposable income.

So, I invite you to take time to read through the extensive content pages, as I ask:

"What is the one biggest hurdle you are facing,
which once resolved,
will make the biggest impact
to both you and your business?"

Chapter One:

Mindset & Motivation

1.7 Living your WHY

We live in a world filled with constant distractions. Endless activities are always floating around us that can take our attention, and often the ones that scream the loudest win. However, a simple way to improve your life is to discover your personal why.

Most people live their lives by focusing on what they must do. The endless tasks continue to mount up, and we wonder why we never feel like we're getting ahead. It feels like we're sprinting on a treadmill just trying to keep up, and every task completed is quickly replaced by new ones.

Life gets a lot simpler when we stop to ask ourselves why we do things.

What Is the Purpose of Your Life?

This is not some big esoteric question that you will ponder for a lifetime. It's just something that you decide for yourself and can change at any time. So, what is the list of most important things to you in your life?

I find it helps to write down things that you **really** love doing. Maybe it's spending time with friends and family, doing a particular hobby, your job, or travelling. But, of course, the answers will be different for every person reading.

What's essential is what's important to you. It's tough to improve your life if you don't know what improvement looks like.

Once you have your initial list, you want to look at what's **important** to you. You do that by asking yourself why you love it and why it's essential to have it in your life. I've been doing this exercise over the last three years and found my list to become more and more refined.

You also want to look at how much time you put into these activities that you love. Do you get to spend as much time as you'd like with each one? Or do they get pushed to the back behind the other tasks in your daily life?

Discovering What's REALLY Important

If you made another list of all the things you are **actually** doing in your life, you'd probably find a bunch of stuff you don't **really** love. For example, some people may hate cooking, and others will love it. Everyone is unique, and this is about finding out what you want to be doing, not what you feel you should be doing.

It's easy to fill our lives with things that don't **really** matter to us. The trick is to ask ourselves how we spend less time doing unimportant things and more time doing what we love. It's not a perfect process where you can drop everything right now, but as you focus from this point on, you'll be amazed at the results.

Always Ask Why

Whenever a new item comes across your plate, you simply ask yourself why. For example, is it imperative to join that new committee for your child's school, or would it be more effective to spend that time with your children instead? Does it matter if you miss your gym time at lunch because your boss needs you to work overtime, or is your fitness break more vital to you?

As I said before, everybody will be different. Some will rank career over fitness, while others will rank it reverse. What matters is that you're making the right choice for yourself.

It May Sound Simple... But That Doesn't Mean It's Easy

Our world is full of expectations placed on us by others... and ourselves. We're expected to be super people who run around and accomplish many different things every day to be great at work and home. As a result, people will often look at you strangely when they ask you how you are, and you don't answer with "busy" with that frantic look in your eye.

However, once you start examining your life through the lens of why, you'll start asking yourself, *"What's important to me?"* Instead, you need to step away from society's expectations and focus on and refine your expectations. When you do this, you'll see the world from an entirely different viewpoint and be free to improve your life in any area that **really** matters to you.

"There's no greater gift than to honour your life's calling. It's why you were born and how you become most truly alive."

Oprah Winfrey

The 10 Benefits of Knowing Your Purpose in Life

1. It helps you stay focused

When you know your life's purpose, it becomes easier to focus on what matters the most in your life. By focusing on one goal, you can find your direction and stay away from distractions.

2. It makes you feel passionate about your goal

Knowing your purpose helps you find your true passion, and passion becomes a vital driver for you to achieve something extraordinary. Whether it is a childhood dream or a newly adopted lifestyle, the desire for it will push you to reach your goals.

3. It gives your life clarity

People who know their purpose in life are unstoppable. This is because they are true to their purpose and shape their life accordingly. On the other hand, people who don't know their purpose in life are unclear about what they want and therefore waste their time on useless things.

4. It makes you feel gratified

When you have a purpose in life, you express it constantly and base your decisions, thoughts, feelings, and actions around that overarching purpose. A person who knows their purpose tends to make a more significant impact through their work, which encourages a sense of gratification.

5. It enables you to live a value-based life

With purpose come values, an integral aspect of a person's life. Values are the rules that guide our decisions in life and help define our goals. They are what tell us when we're on the right path or wrong path and help us find and connect with others who share our way of viewing the world.

"Knowing your purpose in life helps inspire trust in others."

6. It makes you live with integrity

Knowing your purpose in life helps you live life with integrity. People who know their purpose in life know who they are, what they are, and why they are. And when you know yourself, it becomes easier to live a life that's true to your core values.

7. It encourages trust

People who know their purpose report increased synchronicity and serendipity in their lives. With all this comes a deepening of trust and faith in other people; hence they consider themselves an integral part of the universe.

8. It infuses an element of grace in your life

People living their lives with a purpose often report living with grace. This quote by German poet Johann Wolfgang von Goethe sums up the idea and intention at its best: *"Until one commits, there is hesitancy, the chance to draw back, always ineffectiveness."* Yet, amazing things can happen when you commit to living your life with a purpose.

9. It helps you find a flow in life

People who find their purpose tend to live in the flow of the universal stream of consciousness. They allow things to happen and change in their life rather than fighting against it. They tend to challenge themselves and battle against their fears.

10. It makes life even more fun

When people know their purpose in life, they enjoy every minute of it. They can take pleasure in living a purpose-driven life and are better at tackling every situation creatively. Even the dullest thing becomes beautiful and creative when you're motivated by purpose.

Wrapping up

The benefits of living a purpose-driven life are evident. When you live your life with a sense of purpose, you begin living positively and seeking new opportunities. You start experiencing everything that you feel will make a difference.

Relationships are also affected in a positive way when you live life with purpose. You seek out new relationships, nurture the existing ones, and build stronger connections with the people around you. You become more helpful to the people you love and become a role model for your family and friends. You tend to live your life with more curiosity, avoid destructive habits, and seek out good ones that will help you create a difference in the world.

So, if you are still looking for a life purpose, don't put it off any longer. Instead, make it a priority, and you might soon find the peace and serenity that comes from leading a purpose-driven life.

How To Find Your Why and Communicate Your Purpose

All businesses, organizations, and careers operate on three levels:

WHAT we do

HOW we do it

WHY we do it

We're all acquainted with WHAT we do—the products we sell, the services we offer, and our jobs. A few of us know HOW we do it—the things we think differentiate us or make us unique compared to the rest of the crowd or our competition. But only a handful of us can clearly articulate WHY we do what we do...

Our WHY is the purpose, the cause, or the belief that drives every organization and person's career.

WHY does your company exist?

WHY did you get out of bed this morning?

And **WHY** should anyone care?

Your WHY is what sets you apart from everyone else. It's your purpose. It's what inspires you to act. Your WHY inspires others to perform, spread your ideas, or buy your products.

I first learned about this concept of WHY when I read Start with Why by Simon Sinek. In that book, Simon explains how some of the world's most outstanding leaders inspire themselves and others to act, buy their products, or champion their cause.

They do it by clarifying, understanding, and communicating their purpose, their WHY before sharing anything else. They start with, sell with, and lead with WHY.

Sinek's more recent book: Find Your Why, serves as a follow-up to Start with Why.

Whilst Start with Why shows you why it's essential to start with WHY. Finding Your Why shows you how to find your WHY.

Learning to construct a WHY Statement is crucial for discovering your WHY and communicating your purpose to the world. And today, you'll find out exactly how to do it.

Find Your Why and Communicate Your Purpose

Your WHY Statement is the most effective possible way in which you can articulate your WHY—your purpose... Not just to other people, but to yourself as well.

Your WHY Statement should be:
simple and clear, actionable focused on how you'll contribute to others, and expressed in affirmative language that resonates with you

Your WHY statement should be able to encapsulate all the qualities we just mentioned—and it should be able to do so in a single sentence.

It should also be *"evergreen,"* meaning that it should apply to everything you do, both personally and professionally— without separation.

Your WHY Statement is *"A statement of your value at work as much as it is the reason your friends love you. We don't have a professional WHY and a personal WHY. We are who we are, wherever we are. Your contribution is not a product or a service. It's the thing around which everything you do— the decisions you make, the tasks you perform, the products you sell— aligns to bring about the impact you envision."*

The Why Statement Format

Simon and his team provide us with a simple format to use as we draft our WHY Statement:

TO _____ SO THAT _____.

The first blank represents your contribution — the contribution you make to the lives of others through your WHY. And the second blank represents the impact of your contribution.

Your job is to plug in the blanks to create your own unique WHY Statement.

But before you start creating one, it might be helpful to have an example to reference. Here's how Simon Sinek expresses his WHY:

> *"To inspire people to do the things that inspire them so that, together, we can change our world."*

The impact Simon wants is for each of us to change the world. However, we can, for the better. But this alone is too broad. It's incomplete until his intended impact is combined with his contribution—the work he **actually** does on Monday morning to make change happen.

The contribution portion, to inspire people, is what ties it all together, bringing focus and direction to the impact he wants to make on the world. Simon's contribution is essentially WHAT he does (to make his WHY a reality). The books he writes, the workshops he conducts, and the speeches he gives are all part of WHAT he does to move his cause forward—to inspire people to do what motivates them.

And the more he inspires people to do what inspires them, the more of an impact he has towards making the world a better place.

Designated YOU time

You have designated YOU time to allow thinking and self-development

How is the CPD coming along? Are you spending designated time EVERY DAY on YOU and YOUR development?

Interestingly, many studies show that the MORE you try and do, the LESS you achieve. So, this scattergun approach to trying EVERYTHING simply prevents you from ever reaching ANYTHING worthwhile.

I once met a man whose LinkedIn profile showed he was currently employed in 7 different jobs! None of them were interlinked or a natural progression to each other. They were things like R&D tax credit advisor, Juice Distributor, Blog writer, Yoga tutor, etc.

He was exceptionally proud of his profile and asked which of his roles were of most interest to me? And there it was, he had lowered his guard and shown to me he is little more than a *'Jack of all trades, master of none!'*.

I asked him about his wide range of skills and business interests and, after a bit of hesitation, admitted that he had started in all these businesses at one stage or another. However, they hadn't grown to the level of income he required. So *'supplemented'* his income by taking on another *'opportunity'*. When I asked him why he hadn't dropped those that hadn't worked for him to concentrate on his 'new opportunities' he replied, *"But I've already invested some time and money into these. I'd need to recover my time and investment first, and you never know, they might still work!"*.

I was horrified! If there is one lesson to be learnt here, it is:

"If it's going to die, kill it quickly."

There is NOTHING more soul-destroying than allowing a failing business to linger. If you FAIL to invest time (not just at the beginning, but continuously) in YOU and YOUR development, your business WILL stagnate.

"You don't know, WHAT you don't know", Yet it's often NOT knowing that prevents you from making the difference between a win or lose, survive, or die, scale, or grow.

I've spoken at Business Conferences all over the world to business owners of all shapes and sizes. And throughout all my time as a speaker, I can identify three distinct types of business owners in the audience.

There is one group that hang on to your every word. They have notebooks and Dictaphones and take photos of your every slide. I know full well that this group are NOT my ideal target audience! These people will return to their businesses, all fired up and motivated to make the relevant changes from what they have recently learned. However, the following day, REALITY hits when they are back IN the business. Statistics show that only 3% implement what you have taught to the extent that they see a marked change in their business.

Another group, distinctly LACKING at the conference and noticed FOR their absence. These are the ones that are SO BUSY doing the doing; they haven't got time to attend a conference. They might have booked an *'early bird'* ticket (hence noticed by their absence) but are busy DOING and can't spare the time WASTED on potentially NOT learning something new to attend. (These are not my ideal target clients either)

Sadly, the final group (the smallest of the three) ARE my ideal target client.

These are the ones who might not even attend the entire conference! They may arrive late and leave early. However, they have come to listen to ONE or TWO specific speakers because they KNOW exactly WHAT they need to learn and from whom to go away and implement what they have learned.

It's interesting as sometimes you meet these people the day after the conference still at the venue! Whilst everyone else has been in a mad rush to get back and 'implement everything' (only for only 3% of them to do so).

This small bunch of entrepreneurs have strategically planned to stay on AFTER the event to PLAN what they have learned and HOW it shall be implemented.

Interestingly I read once about an employer that INSISTED that for every four days you worked IN the business, you had to take at least ½ a day to work on YOU. It didn't matter if that was reading, walking, climbing, shopping, or sitting in a coffee shop people watching, but it did matter that you did it EVERY week!

I read it as part of a news bio on the company that had just won one of the FTSE 500 fastest-growing start-ups, and the Entrepreneur owner was being interviewed about his 'overnight success'. He attributed ALL the success to the strength, commitment, and FREE WILL of the people within and exclaimed:

> *"I'm not that smart,*
> *I'm just smart enough to recognise who is"*

There is a FABULOUS quote from Einstein I refer to often when people tell me they haven't got the time to study, to learn to improve themselves.

"You will NEVER overcome any problem in life, whilst using the same level of thinking as that which caused the problem. If I had one day to save the world, I'd spend the first 23Hours thinking about how to save the world!"

And another from my Great grandmother, who sadly passed slightly after her 103 birthday.

On her hundredth birthday celebration, I'd asked what she attributed such a successful and meaningful life? She replied, *"I've always remained active and have never gone to bed without learning something new!"*

1.8 Building a Winning Team

Rome wasn't built in a day, and neither shall your sustainable scaleup business. Far too many business owners become the bottleneck in their own business's success, by failing to hire early enough, and when they do, hiring the wrong people!

Your role as the business owner, is to make yourself 'surplus to requirement' as quickly as possible. By recruiting and then delegating the doing of the business to others.

Yet too many owners retain the mindset that *"nobody can do what I do"* or *"But they can't do it as well as me"* as apposed to breaking each task they are doing and then asking the question:

*"Who do I know, that **could** do this?"*

Yes, there may be some training, mentoring, coaching required so that they can do this. But **that** is the role of an entrepreneur **not** doing the doing (Or building an empire where you are still central to its ongoing success!)

1.9 Income at will generators

There is a HUGE difference, almost immeasurable, between working HARD and working SMART. The wealthiest people alive these days often DO little, but this is often deceiving, as hundreds are doing the REAL work, thousands, even tens of thousands of others to which they receive a benefit.

There has always been those who 'generate income at will'. However, in the older, more traditional sense, this wasn't achieved until you had built a business empire where many others were working tirelessly for a business to which you are the majority shareholder and benefited from a very profitable dividend.

However, since the evolution of the internet, this doesn't have to be the case and has given rise to a new form of income at will generation – Automated ONLINE sales.

It has now never been easier to make money whilst you sleep with little to no effort by you whatsoever (once the systems and processes are in place)

Let's take Bradley, for example. Bradley is a 22-year-old single male still living with his family and starting his entrepreneurial journey. With an 'average' educational background and 'average' grades, under the older working method, Bradley would be destined for an 'average' job working in an 'average' environment, earning an 'average' wage WHILST generating a residual income for the business owner.

However, since leaving mainstream education, Bradley has self-studied AUTOMATION. Or, in more lay terms – How to get a computer and the internet to generate an income for him WITHOUT BEING PRESENT!

Bradley has learnt all about Chatbots. The little pop-up that appears on more and more web pages asking if you need any help? Initially, this used to (and in some places still does) connect you to a human being working in the company who stopped what they were doing to type to you, as opposed to you having to call and speak to them! However, as Bot technology improved, the Bot could be pre-programed to recognise Frequently Asked Questions and respond to these without the need for human intervention. This was a significant step forward but still required the Bot to be programmed with the responses

and could only answer questions asked before. However, the most recent breakthroughs in technology are LearnerBots. A Chatbot that observes EVERY keystroke of the operator within the business and 'learns' their language, mannerisms, and style can replicate this to mimic human intervention.

Take this a stage further, and Google Voice can make and receive calls, take orders, and pay using an automated human simulated voice (including accents and the occasional bit of humour!)

With a one-off set-up fee and a fraction of the actual cost of employing someone to take the pizza order, taxi request, hotel reservation, you can now have an automated human simulated voice bot doing the work for you!

Being a Chatbot specialist and being able to sell the service to the end-user and program the bot, install it, and charge a monthly management fee for it to remain in place. As a result, Bradley can generate a small income from hundreds and hundreds of clients whilst not doing any further work.

YES, he must be available to call if a computer glitch occurs and there is a problem....
However, there's an automated ticketing helpdesk for that!
And deems he only works when he chooses!

The other MAJOR benefit of this way of working is RISK!

As an employee, you commit EVERYTHING you have to one employer. Sometimes this is contractual; other times, simply deeming to take on another P/T job at best is all they can do.

Likewise, as a Business Owner, we look to SHARE the risk by having multiple clients.

In this extended RISK SHARING model, charging such a small monthly fee is unlikely to cause the client ever to wish to cancel. But instead, sharing the risk between thousands of clients, whilst NOT increasing the hours (beyond initial set up), enables a sustainable lifestyle with little ongoing WORK, mitigating the risk if a client cancels. This subsequently has such a low impact on HIM.

With Google predicting more than $1Bn a year and will continue to be spent on ONLINE LEARNING, there has never been a better opportunity to share your expertise with others. By putting the HARD WORK in now to build a value proposition and subsequently receive a regular income from others benefiting from you sharing that expertise for a notional fee compared to having you 1:1 in the room with them.

The most significant MISTAKE people make is in valuing their online content. YES, it is of massive value, and NO, you shouldn't simply be giving it away. However, there is a HUGE difference between BESPOKE 1:1 intervention and the more mainstream non-bespoke content suitable for a larger

audience. Therefore, don't be greedy, be willing to receive a fraction of the bespoke investment requirement in ONLINE payments to attract a far larger ongoing global digital audience.

Furthermore, the considerable increase in affiliate marketing has seen another surge in those making a significant income without doing much work! In our series of 6 #ADDAZERO Activator Workshops[1], we identify how anyone can achieve a 7-figure annual income by offering to the right people at the right price and applying LEVERAGE.

How can YOU benefit on an ongoing basis from leveraging OTHER people's clients to sell OTHER people's products/services, sometimes by utilising OTHER people's MONEY to do so!

Let's take a well-known insurance comparison website!

Since the demise of insurance brokerages, the business plan showed that many people were ill-informed about the variety and breadth of insurance companies and policies available to them, often resulting in either paying too much for the insurance they required OR being under insurance. As a result, there was a niche for a comparative website to bring all options together. Allowing the consumer may be more reliably informed about their opportunities.

There was a significant 'build' cost of such a website and the need for an affiliate agreement to be set up, managed, and maintained. So that each insurance provider to be displayed.

---

[1] 1/2 Day training workshops designed to support Business Owners to identify and overcome the hurdles **every** business face when looking to Scale. For further details, visit: www.mytruenorth.biz/events

Therefore, an investor (in this case, a Venture Capitalist) was sought to cover the cost of the initial expenditure (other people's MONEY). Once the site was built, it would also need EVERYONE to know about it, so a further investment was required to run a substantial national marketing campaign alerting the potential consumers as to its availability and the benefits to the end-user. This was achieved through associate marketing – partnering with others with HUGE lists of their ideal target consumer clients (Other people's CLIENTS).

Once the site went live and the enquiries (and orders) began to come through, the services were being provided by the insurance companies (other people's PRODUCTS/SERVICES) for which they received a small percentage of commission, which in the early days was split between further marketing costs and repaying the VC.

The business made NO money for several years (whilst the VC was being repaid). In the knowledge that ONCE the investment was repaid, if the marketing costs remained in place, the money which had been paid to the VC was now PROFIT!

Income at will - Advanced

Your covers all your outgoings and living expenses before starting work.

It's one thing to manage to achieve this whilst you have limited outgoings, at the start of the journey. However, as the business grows, so do your own expenses. However, ensuring you have sufficient income generated when you continuously work enables you to approach EVERYTHING with an entirely different level of aptitude and attitude.

I recall several years ago now, sitting with an entrepreneur discussing his X and Y figures!

His X figure (moved every year, dependent on his children's age, where they wanted to go on holiday, whether a new car was required or any home renovation work, etc.) X = the figure the family need each year to do everything they want to do, without compromise. It wasn't just the holidays, though; it was the upgraded flights, the concerts and away days they wanted. It took into consideration EVERY DAY of expenditure for the next 12 months. And his primary role in January was to ensure the business could deliver that to THEIR income over the next 12 months.

You see:

> *"Your business is a resource."*

And just like my spectacles, my mobile phone, and my car. It MUST be fit for purpose.

However, he then went on to talk about his Y figure. The amount of money he would require, to maintain his X figure

FOR THE REST OF HIS LIFE. Suppose he or the business ceased to operate! How much HE would need in HIS bank account that his family could enjoy the life they had become accustomed to IF either HE or the business were NO MORE.

I know we should all have life insurance and protection plans. But invariably, these are set against financial commitments such as mortgages, loans, DEBTS and not considered regarding the FUTURE lifestyle.

How much money do you need for TODAY, for THIS YEAR, for the next 5 YEARS?

How much additional money does your family require for the rest of your life, IF the worst were to happen?

Only once you know you have these bases covered can you talk about Financial Freedom. Yet, so many people fall short of either giving this the consideration it is due or keeping it up to date as you and your business continue to progress!

Want Versus Need

You are not prevented from doing what you want by things you 'HAVE' to do

The chances are good that, at some time in your life, you've taken a time management class, read about it in books, and tried to use an electronic or paper-based day planner to organize, prioritize and schedule your day. "Why, with this knowledge and these gadgets," you may ask, "do I still feel like I can't get everything done I need to?"

The answer is simple. Everything you ever learned about managing time is a complete waste of time because it doesn't work.

Before you can even begin to manage time, you must learn what time is. A dictionary defines time as "the point or period at which things occur." So, put simply, time is when stuff happens.

There are two types of time: clock time and real-time. In clock time, there are 60 seconds in a minute, 60 minutes in an hour, 24 hours in a day and 365 days in a year. All-time passes equally. When someone turns 50, they are exactly 50 years old, no more or no less.

In real-time, all time is relative. Time flies or drags, depending on what you're doing. Two hours stuck on the hard shoulder awaiting recovery can feel like 12 years. And yet our 12-year-old children seem to have grown up in only two hours.

Spring-Cleaning Tips for Your Business

Which time describes the world in which you really live, real-time or clock time?

The reason time management gadgets and systems don't work are that these systems are designed to manage clock time. Clock time is irrelevant. You don't live in or even have access to clock time. You live in real-time, a world in which all time flies when you are having fun or drags when you are doing your taxes.

The good news is that real-time is mental. It exists between your ears. You create it. Anything you make, you can manage. It's time to remove any self-sabotage or self-limitation you have around "*not having enough time*" or today not being "*the right time*" to start a business or manage your current business properly.

There are only three ways to spend time: thoughts, conversations, and actions. Regardless of the type of business you own, your work will be composed of those three items.

As an entrepreneur, you may be frequently interrupted or pulled in different directions. While you cannot eliminate interruptions, you do get a say on how much time you will spend on them and how much time you will spend on the thoughts, conversations and actions that will lead you to success.

Tips for a More Productive Day

Practice the following techniques to become the master of your own time:

1. Carry a schedule and record all your thoughts, conversations, and activities for a week. This will help you understand how much you can get done during a day and where your precious moments are going. You'll see how much time is spent producing results

and how much time is wasted on unproductive thoughts, conversations, and actions.

2. Any activity or conversation that's important to your success should have time assigned to it. To-do lists get longer and longer to the point where they're unworkable. Appointment books work. Schedule appointments with yourself and create time blocks for high-priority thoughts, conversations, and actions. Schedule when they will begin and end. Have the discipline to keep these appointments. Plan to spend at least 50 per cent of your time engaged in the thoughts, activities and conversations that produce most of your results.

3. Schedule time for interruptions. Plan time to be pulled away from what you're doing. Take, for instance, the concept of having "*office hours*." Of course, this isn't actually "office hours" merely another way of saying "planned interruptions?"

4. Take the first 30 minutes of every day to plan your day. Don't start your day until you complete your time plan. The most crucial time of your day is the time you schedule to schedule time.

5. Take five minutes before every call and task to decide what result you want to attain. This will help you know what success looks like before you start. And it will also slow time down. Next, take five minutes after each call and activity to determine whether your desired result was achieved. If not, what was missing? Finally, how do you put what's missing in your next call or activity?

6. Put up a **"Do not disturb"** sign when you must get work done. Practice not answering the phone just because it's ringing and e-mails just because they show up. Disconnect instant messaging. Don't instantly give people your attention unless it's crucial in your business to offer an immediate human response. Instead, schedule a time to answer emails and return phone calls. Block out other distractions like Facebook and other forms of social media unless you use these tools to generate business.

Remember that it's impossible to get everything done. But also remember that odds are good that 20 per cent of your thoughts, conversations and activities produce 80 per cent of your results.

Time Management for Entrepreneurs

There are two things you need to conquer if you want to enable time freedom, and here I've listed them both.

Firstly, you are likely to HATE me and wish you'd NEVER started because for one day. I want you to record your day HONESTLY and ACCURATELY!

When I say HONESTLY, I mean record EVERYTHING you do, and ACCURATELY I mean the time it takes you to do it!

EXAMPLE

03.47Hrs Woke to use the bathroom –
Remembered I need to send an email to X 03.53 am returned to bed.

23.51Hrs Lighted out and headed to bed. – Remembered I STILL need to send an email to X and add it to my TO-DO list for tomorrow!

The last time I did this (I do it at least once a year), I recorded over 1000 actions within a 24Hr period. (And yes, it was one of my least productive days all year!)

However, the next step is to take three colour pens!

[For the sake of this book being printed in Black and White, and for those with colour blindness, I'm not going to stipulate WHAT colours you need, but for the sake of argument in this context, we are going to use Red, Green and Blue.]

Step 1 – RED PEN

Take the red pen and underscore EVERY task you completed that day, that you still WANT to be doing in the next 12,24,36Months!

WOW, when you REALLY do this, have you seen how LITTLE Red ink you've used! That's amazing. Straight away we've identified a whole ton of 'stuff' you're currently doing that you really shouldn't be!

"Stop doing £10 tasks, at the risk of missing £1000 opportunities"

Step 2 – BLUE PEN

Now with the Blue Pen, highlight every task you COULD get somebody else to do IF you asked, told, taught, paid to do so! – DO NOT simply give tasks to other people, so they are not on your list. Instead, consider each task in turn and determine who is the RIGHT person to give this to, based on their skills, abilities, attributes, personality etc.

Step 3 – GREEN PEN

Any task left un-marked is a task that might need to be outsourced! Outsourcing NON-business-critical tasks is an excellent way of ensuring they still get done to an acceptable standard WHILST you concentrate on the RED PEN tasks!

Yes, there may well be a need to ASK some people to do things, maybe tell some people to do some extra things, or train them or even re-numerate them accordingly. But the fact is, we've freed you up from the things you shouldn't be doing, concentrating on the things you really should!

I've been doing this for years, within my own business. And with the hundreds if not thousands of business owners, I've also encouraged to do it. I've found:

1.   You initially highlight less than 12% of the list

2.   The added costs of either training, re-numerating, or outsourcing only determine you need to do between 17-23% more of the things you SHOULD be doing to cover the cost of the additional expenditure!

3.   This leaves more than 60% additional revenue potential if you simply concentrate on the tasks only you should be doing!

The 4 D's of Effective Management

WHENEVER ANYTHING either lands on your desk, in your inbox, or on the phone, you apply the 4D's before doing anything else!

1.   **DELETE** – Has this got ANYTHING to do with You, Your Family, Your Business or Your goals? I find more and more time is being wasted 'helping' others to achieve their goals, AT THE COST of you ever reaching yours!

2. **DELEGATE** – Who is the RIGHT person to be dealing with this task? I can almost guarantee they have asked you because they Know, Like and Trust YOU. However, are YOU the RIGHT person to do this, or simply the conduit between problem and solution.

3. **DEFFER** – Just because it's URGENT to them doesn't automatically mean it's urgent to you. If it can't be DELETED or DELEGATED, then WHEN is the right time for YOU to do this?

4. **DO** – We only accept URGENT work to DO if it's brought to us by somebody else. Otherwise, it hits the defer pile and is attended to WHEN it's essential to us!

This might appear harsh but try it. You'd be AMAZED at how much time you get back and what you can now be doing with it.!

1.10 Time freedom

You have the right team around you, ensuring you spend your time doing the RIGHT things. Rome wasn't built in a day but by an army of people working towards a common purpose.

"The greatest investment a business owner can EVER make is in the recruitment and development of its people"

Bill Gates

If you consider almost every scale business for one moment, the most significant ongoing investment is SALARY. The costs are associated with having a TEAM to manage and maintain the business.

Get this RIGHT, and it proves to be an excellent investment. Can you take me to any investment broker or bookie who can repeatedly generate 250%, 300%, 350%+ ROI MONTHLY on your investment? The simple answer is – YOU CAN'T. By far, investment in people has GOT TO BE the BEST investment you can possibly EVER make – **WHEN YOU GET IT RIGHT!**

The problem is, how do you know who is right?

Well, for that, we must come back to Vision, Values, Culture, Purpose, as we spoke about at the start of this journey.

Finding, recruiting, maintaining BRILLIANT staff within any business is a FULL TIME (with overtime) job. The ONLY way to manage a highly successful business is to manage a highly successful team. That means your role becomes HOW to find, recruit, and maintain brilliance at work. EVERYDAY.

"Until you have an employee…. you are one!"

It might appear cruel, but it's true. Until you have someone capable of either generating an income or supporting you in generating MORE income, you are simply SELF EMPLOYED!

Yet getting the right mix of income generators and support staff, ensuring all of them are working at their prime, doing the best they can do, with a common aim to achieve more for the business, is a tireless task.

Hiring the right employee is a challenging process. Hiring the wrong employee is expensive, costly to your work environment, and time-consuming. But, on the other hand, hiring the right employee pays you back in employee productivity, a successful employment relationship, and a positive impact on your total work environment.

Hiring the right employee enhances your work culture and pays you back a thousand times over in high employee morale, positive, forward-thinking planning, and accomplishing challenging goals. It also ensures that you are making the most of the time and energy your other employees invest in a relationship with the new employee—a costly and emotional process.

You can learn a lot more about Recruiting, Retaining, and Rewarding Superhero's in the final chapter of this book: Winning Team.

1.11 Abundance

You are creating an abundance for others and are giving back.

Far too many busy business owners dismiss charity as something 'others' do. Or at best throw £20 at those asking for support as they are 'too busy building their own business.

Others are a little more charitable in nature and have great plans for all the giving they shall be doing **once** they have achieved success (*Sound familiar?*)

I've got some bad news for you – The world doesn't work like that! And until you learn **this** important lesson, there is likely no real reason to continue reading this book and hoping to scale!

You see, you must **be** the person you **want** to become! Too many people have heard the expression *Fake it, till you make it* and think that gives them permission to lie, cheat, steal – posting fake news and (what's quickly becoming known as Airbnb fame) by those hiring glamorous apartment for a insta photoshoot whilst claiming to have hit the elusive 7 figure milestone!

No - Fake it, till ya make it is **not** what I'm referring to here.

However, you do need to '*step into*' the person you intend to be. You have to have already determined what the future successful business owner looks like, smells like! What they do, say, listen to, eat etc. And if that future super successful business owner is charitable, then in order for you to become that person, you have to start **now**.

I'm proud to share we are members of the B1G1 – Global Giving Community. Through which ALL of our actions are aligned with the UN 17 Global Sustainability Goals by giving to good causes.
And, by having purchased a copy of **this book** you have also enabled us to make a donation through B1G1 to provide entrepreneur education to micro business start up's. you can learn more by visiting http://bit.ly/exploreb1g1 (and, if your inspired to join also, use the code: BM14841. As when you join through our code, 50 days of access to education are given to children in the world.

If you would like to learn even more about the information within this chapter, there are 3 exceptional other books I'd certainly and most happily recommend.

The first is possible THE business book, I have read more times than ANY other. EVERY time I read this; I still learn something new. I'm talking about **"Rich Dad, Poor Dad"** *by Robert Kiyosaki.* I strongly recommend this should stay close, it has and continues to serve me well.

The second book is **"The compound effect"** *by Darren Hardy.* This is a great read on understanding more about how a series of little things once put together and repeat again and again and again. Continually looking at, tweaking, improving can go on to have such an INCREDIBLE long-term impact.

And finally, **"The Millionaire Masterplan"** *by Roger J. Hamilton.* An excellent read for anyone wanting to understand more about how to think differently and the impact of leverage.

Chapter two:

Vision, Values, Culture, Purpose

2.5 Category of ONE

Any company should strive not to become a leader in a category, but to create a new category altogether and be the only company in it. To accomplish this, a company must make a purposeful decision, and that decision must be followed with action. The company must let go of past success and strive for more; everyone involved must be committed to this new direction.

Business leaders should therefore take the following advice:

- A company must have a story – a purpose for existing beyond producing a product or providing a service. This becomes the guiding force behind everything everyone in the company does.
- Because the business world itself changes so frequently, businesses need to become accustomed to constant change and not become complacent. Otherwise, they run the risk of disappearing.
- To transcend commodity, a company must defy comparison in the customer's eyes. It is not possible to create a great company through advertising, and false promises do not fool consumers.
- A company's brand is most important, and the customer defines it. Companies must recognize that their brand is everything: who they are, what they promise to deliver, and how often they make good on that promise.

If a company is competitive with price, quality, and service, then following three customer rules should put that company on the path to becoming a Category of One business:
1. know more about the customer
2. get closer to the customer
3. emotionally connect with the customer better than anyone else.

Not only is the customer always right, but now the customer also makes the rules and runs the game; successful companies embrace this fact. Delivering on the basics – price, product, service, and quality – every time with each and every customer could very well be the differentiating factor that sets a company apart from its competition.

Why it pays to create a Category

People have been brewing coffee for more than 500 years, but if you go into a kitchen today to look at how it's made, you'll probably see a process that bears little resemblance to the methods used just a generation ago. In homes and businesses alike, consumers are shifting to the cup-at-a-time pod-style brewing as an alternative to the messy communal office coffeepot.

Pod Brewing now come in more than 200 flavours and sell for about 10 times the cost per cup of coffee brewed by traditional methods, but consumers are willing to pay for the experience. In 2012 U.K. sales of pod-style coffeemakers and pods exceeded £137M. This increase in popularity is having a huge impact on sales of coffee pods with value up by an impressive 29.6% on the previous year (correct at time of publication)

To find out just how lucrative category creation can be, Harvard Business Review examined Fortune's lists of the 100 fastest-growing companies from 2009 to 2011. They found that the 13 companies that were instrumental in creating their categories accounted for 53% of incremental revenue growth and 74% of incremental market capitalization growth over those three years.

The message is clear: Category creators experience much faster growth and receive much higher valuations from investors than companies bringing only incremental innovations to market.

New Categories, Outsize Growth
Sometimes category creation involves dreaming up a new class
of products that can be sold using traditional methods.
Consider Kevin Plank's creation of Under Armour, $1 billion–
plus brands that used new fabrics to reinvent the way
consumers think about girdles and T-shirts. Or Chobani, which
created a market for thicker, creamier, high-protein yogurt—a
market that's now in the range of $1 billion annually and has
drawn multiple competitors.

More often, though, category creation involves both a
breakthrough product and a breakthrough business model.
Examples include Microsoft's Xbox Live gaming system, which
combines a traditional video game with a subscription-based
online service and Vistaprint, a web-based print shop that goes
beyond traditional stationery to create marketing brochures,
and promotional items such as iPhone covers and drink
sleeves.

How to Create a Category
Unfortunately, though, category creation is the exception for
large companies, not the rule. According to data in Nielsen's
Breakthrough Innovation Report, only 13% of the world's
leading consumer product companies introduced a
breakthrough innovation from 2008 to 2010—and even fewer
created a breakthrough business model as well. Although large
companies have the resources, capabilities, and growth
aspirations to drive category creation, many market leaders
merely sit on the side-lines watching new entrants create
breakthrough products and business models. When Harvard
Business Review polled senior executives why their
organizations don't pursue category creation, they got the
same three answers.

1. **Start-ups are better at creating breakthrough innovations.**

Which is a fallacy. Apple was more than 20 years old when it launched iTunes, the key innovation that allowed it to shift from computers to consumer electronics and media. The only thing keeping most big companies from creating new categories is their lack of imagination—their inability to see beyond what they're selling today.

Some of that lack of imagination stems from organizational issues. One CEO put it: "*I'd love to work on category creation, but who would I give the assignment to? My existing team are running the regular business, and my innovation team is focused on finding new products in our current categories.*" In such situations, we usually advise companies to build elite short-term teams focused on category creation. Make it a six-month assignment for high performers from marketing, sales, finance, and operations. Give them the funding they need for research and travel, along with the opportunity to present their findings to top executives. Using this process, GE Healthcare created an ultra-portable, low-cost, easy-to-use ultrasound machine for the Chinese market.

2. **We can't afford to do this.**

Perhaps the most prevalent misperception is that creating a new category requires a huge incremental expense. In fact, companies can often find opportunities by using their existing budgets more efficiently. Very often, the most important work involves coming up with an insight about an unmet consumer need. Many companies devote too much of their market research budgets to understanding the current market; according to a 2009 study by a Business Consulting Group, only

20% to 35% of budgets are spent on strategic, forward-looking studies. They concluded this should be at least 50%.

3. Our market is mature; our customers don't want to try new things.

When a company is selling a product that's been around forever, it may have a hard time believing that consumers have a hidden desire or an untapped need that the product isn't satisfying. But the world is full of examples of long-established everyday products that were disrupted by better mousetraps—and smart leaders are on a constant search to ensure that their companies come up with the mousetraps. One example is the Oral-B Pulsar, a battery-powered toothbrush launched by Gillette's Oral-B division in 2004. The toothbrush market had been split into two distinct categories—manual toothbrushes that cost around £1, and plug-in electric ones that cost £50 or more.

Oral-B research uncovered latent demand among consumers who took pride in the active cleaning required by a manual toothbrush and didn't want the "*autopilot*" experience of a high-end electric brush but might be open to a hybrid. The team began to imagine a new, "super-premium-manual" category of disposable brushes, which would cost about £5-8 and still require a user to actively brush but would provide a power boost. (One team member dubbed the product "the moped of toothbrushes.") During its first year the Pulsar earned £70million in revenue—and the growth it provided was a factor in Procter & Gamble's $57 billion purchase of Gillette.

The Pulsar illustrates another essential point about category creation: Sometimes, potential breakthrough innovations have already been manufactured but are waiting for a creative, energetic leader to take note. Successful category creators don't get hung up on who invented a concept if they can find a way to harness it themselves.

First, get the right people into jobs that allow them to look well beyond the markets you currently serve.

Second, conduct a market research audit, focusing on whether you're spending too much on understanding existing trends and your own market and too little on trying to predict future behaviour and looking to adjacencies. (Most companies are guilty on both counts.)

Third, think creatively about resources and incentives. Consider establishing a budget for category creation and make it clear that you're willing to invest in ideas that may not offer big short-term profits but could move the company into new spaces.

Finally, remember that risk aversion keeps many companies from creating new categories. Take a hard look at your company's culture and make sure you're not one of them—the rewards of launching a new category are simply too great.

2.6 The E-Myth Principles

It doesn't matter who, where or what you do within your business. If you are serious about modern day entrepreneurship and applying its principles. In that case, you should, in some part, be grateful for the impact Mr Michael E. Gerber has played in shaping what we know to be the life and role of an entrepreneur. For me, he is one of the forefathers of modern-day entrepreneurs, and his book the E-Myth, the backbone on which most new businesses are often now formed.

Gerber's New York Times, Wall Street Journal, and Business Week best-selling books of all time have touched the lives of millions of readers throughout the world. Inc. Magazine called him 'the World's #1 Small Business Guru'. He started over 40 years ago by addressing a significant need in the small business market: businesses owned primarily by people with technical skills but few entrepreneurial skills.

What is the E-Myth Principles?
Well, ultimately, it boils down to two distinct points:
1. Working ON the business, not IN the business
2. Building a world-class team

The book is presented as a series of conversations with Sarah, a fictional small business owner whom the author is mentoring. He quickly identifies, 'Sarah' is spending so much time working IN the business, she fails to allow herself the time, energy, effort, or consideration to work ON the business. And by spending time working ON the most important things to her in the advancement of her business, rather than 'not having the time'. It enables her to take on a team and thus progress the company by more and more on it.

Blocking out designated time daily and weekly to specifically work ON the business is essential if you want to continue to SCALE. Gerber also remarked, *"Until you have an employee, you are one"*, Which, whilst a little blunt, is also very true. You must ensure you regularly block out time **for you**. That could be to review and revise a specific business element, go out and win new business, build relationships with suppliers, partners, or your referral network. Or even to work on your health, nutrition, fitness. Growing a more significant business determines you must grow also.

That means putting **YOU** at the top of the TODO list to ensure your number one priority is being at your best, so you can deliver the best to the business.

2.7 Audacious Goals

What I find particularly fascinated when we get to this level of detail within the Vision, Values, Culture, Purpose, of a business is if we have begun to 'play safe'. You see, by now you will already have seen a marked difference in Why we do what we do and HOW we do what we do. And this recognition isn't just being observed inside the business, but outside also. It's hugely important to remain on top of this because it is THE foundation on which we are building EVERYTHING else.

However, how many times have you come across the term working SMARTER, or SMART goals and objectives? SMART is being used here as an acronym. Used to represent the 6 considerations many corporate and public sector employers put into the Key Performance Indicators (KPI's) of their employees.

> **S** – Specific. There should never be a goal set that isn't clear as to exactly what is required, and how the results of whether it has been delivered are being recorded.
> **M** – Measurable. I've already mentioned the word results being recorded, so how we measure the success or work towards to success.
> **A** - Achievable. The goals set should be within the persons capacity and capability to achieve, both in terms of ability and time.
> **R** – Realistic. There are little point setting goals which are unrealistic to achieve. We would all 'like' it done by yesterday, but clearly that's not possible.
> **T** – Time bound. Unless there is a timeframe, a deadline set for these goals, we may well never achieve them and

simply claim to still be working towards achieving them! Therefore, TIME must be included to determine WHAT is going to be achieved, BY whom, to WHAT standard and BY when.

All in all, it sounds very familiar to most, and fair?

However, there is also a huge argument as to why as a business owner you should NEVER set SMART objectives! Either for yourself or especially for the business! For this to be explained, I must first remind you:

"You don't know, what you don't know"

Kolb's first defined the four stages of competence as:
1. Unconscious incompetence
2. Conscious incompetence
3. Conscious competence
4. Unconscious competence

Put more simply:
1. We don't know that we don't know
2. We now realise, we don't know
3. We learn to know
4. We know

Using this as a framework to challenge the SMART methodology. Why would we ever set personal or business targets that are REALISTIC and ACHIEVEABLE! The business of business is business. Or more simply, the main purpose of business is to grow and prosper that **everyone** within may benefit by doing so. (Yes, it's a more modern and holistic view by stating EVERYONE rather than business owners, but hey, that's what you get for reading a book written by the founder of the Ethical Coaching Company!)

Based on Kolb, that clearly shows we would only set objectives and goals that are within our current level of thinking, and yet it is already established we don't know, what we don't know. Therefore, by setting goals within our current understanding we are by default NOT thinking of all the things the business COULD achieve but as of, yet we are not aware of!

My good friend – David Hyner spent years interviewing people at the very TOP of their profession. From politicians to popstars and every walk of life between the two to gain a greater understanding on how they have achieved SO much more than all their competitors. In well over 250 interviews, not ONE of them spoke of Achievable, Realistic goals. They all spoke passionately about their VISON which involved something so audacious that when their first set out they had NO IDEA as to how or if it would ever be possible. They took the Martin Luther King quote literally "I had a dream..." and they went for it. They were ALL in on a belief system that ultimately overcame whatever hurdles may have otherwise been in the way. Their audacity to think BIG was also their saviour from thinking SMALL!

Therefore, SMART goals are rather DUMB!

Or perhaps they OUGHT to be!

Have you ever heard of DUMB goals? I hadn't until I watched public speaker and author of the book motivation manifesto – Brendan Burchard.
Both Dave Hyner and Brendon Burchard say instead, of SMART goals, we should set our sights much higher and focus on changing the world.

According to both Dave and Brendon, these are goals that are:

- **D**ream driven
- **U**plifting
- **M**ethod friendly
- **B**ehaviour driven

But where do you start?

Well, not wanting to take anything away from either Dave or Brendan we've come up with our own take on this, and it's called BFHAG!

That's a goal so big, fat, and hairy that if you don't stop everything right now and concentrate every effort you have from now until you achieve it, there is little chance you will ever achieve it. Make it very specific (in terms of a clear target and a clear deadline) and ensure it impacts EVERYONE who will be in any way associated with it, beyond you, and your immediate family. Ensure it has such appeal that everyone who hears, see's, learns of it, either buys it from you or wants to be a part of creating it (and preferably both!)

What impact can you have on the world?

Once you have that, and you share it with one person and they simply say "Wow, REALLY?" then you know your close to devising YOUR BFHAG!

So, what I'd like you to do, as we begin to close this chapter, is on the following page (left blank on purpose) for you to write down THE most outrageously audacious goal you can possibly conceive, by answering this question:

If neither time or money were an objection
(you have all the time and money in the world)
What would you do?

There is a very well-known powerful book which may help you find absolute clarity in all that you are aiming to achieve here. It's *by Steven Covey* entitled: **The 7 Habits of highly effective people.**

When Stephen Covey first released The Seven Habits of Highly Effective People, the book became an instant rage because people suddenly got up and took notice that their lives were headed off in the wrong direction; and more than that, they realized that there were so many simple things they could do to navigate their life correctly.

Another book you might find Powerful, especially when looking to pass over any responsibility you have previously maintained to other people within your growing business, is **Chimp Paradox** *by Professor Steve Peters.*

Leading consultant psychiatrist Steve Peters knows more than anyone how impulsive behaviour or nagging self-doubt can impact negatively on our professional and personal lives.

There is also a fabulous book entitled **Category of One - How Extraordinary Companies Transcend Commodity and Defy Comparison** by *Joe Calloway.*

Full of case studies and personal reflections by leaders of exceptional companies, this book is designed to help anyone transform their run-of-the-mill business into an extraordinary company. Simple lessons that lead to real, proven results.

And of course, if you haven't already read it, you really should own a copy of **the E-Myth** (The original was written and published in 1986 but was updated and re-written **'The E-Myth, revisited'** in 1995.

Chapter Three:

Strategy & Structure

3.7 7 Key Models for Growth

A growth strategy involves more than simply envisioning long-term success. If you don't have a tangible plan, you're losing business -- or you're increasing the chance of losing business to competitors.

The key with any growth strategy is to be deliberate. Figure out the rate-limiting step in your growth and pour as much fuel on the fire as possible.

But for this to be beneficial, you need to take the following steps:

1. Establish a value proposition

For your business to sustain long-term growth, you must understand what sets it apart from the competition. Identify why customers come to you for a product or service.

What makes you relevant, differentiated, and credible? Use your answer to explain to other consumers why they should do business with you.

For example, some companies compete on "authority" -- Whole Foods Market is the definitive place to buy healthy, organic foods. Others, such as Walmart, compete on price. Figure out what special benefit only you can provide and forget everything else. If you stray from this proposition, you'll only run the risk of devaluing your business.

2. Identify your ideal customer

You got into business to solve a problem for a certain audience. Who is that audience? Is that audience your ideal customer? If not, who are you serving? Nail down your ideal customer and revert to this audience as you adjust business to stimulate growth.

3. Define your key indicators

Changes must be measurable. If you're unable to measure a change, you have no way of knowing whether it's effective. Identify which key indicators affect the growth of your business, then dedicate time and money to those areas. Also, A/B test properly -- making changes over time and comparing historical and current results isn't valid.

4. Verify your revenue streams

What are your current revenue streams? What revenue streams could you add to make your business more profitable?

Once you identify the potential for new revenue streams, ask yourself if they're sustainable in the long run. Some great ideas or cool products don't necessarily have revenue streams attached. Be careful to isolate and understand the difference.

5. Look to your competition

No matter your industry, your competition is likely excelling at something that your company is struggling with. Look toward similar businesses that are growing in new, unique ways to inform your growth strategy. Don't be afraid to ask for advice. Ask yourself why your competitors have made alternate choices. Are they wrong? Or are your businesses positioned differently? The assumption that you're smarter is rarely correct.

6. Focus on your strengths

Sometimes, focusing on your strengths -- rather than trying to improve your weaknesses -- can help you establish growth strategies. Reorient the playing field to suit your strengths and build upon them to grow your business.

7. Invest in talent

Your employees have direct contact with your customers, so you need to hire people who are motivated and inspired by your company's value proposition. Be cheap with office furniture, marketing budgets and holiday parties. Hire few employees but pay them way above the industry average. The best ones will stick around if you need to cut back their compensation during a slow period.

Developing a growth strategy isn't a one-size-fits-all process. In fact, due to changing market conditions, making strategic decisions based on someone else's successes would be foolish. That's not to say that you can't learn from another company, but blindly implementing a cookie-cutter plan won't create sustainable growth.

You need to adapt your plan to smooth out your business's inefficiencies, refine its strengths and better suit your customers - who could be completely different than those from a vague, one-size-fits-all strategy.

Your company's data should lend itself to all your strategic decisions. Specifically, you can use the data from your key indicators and revenue streams to create a personalized growth plan. That way, you'll better understand your business and your customers' nuances, which will naturally lead to growth.

A one-size-fits-all strategy implies vague indicators. But a specific plan is a successful plan. When you tailor your growth strategy to your business and customers, you'll keep your customers happy and fulfil their wants and needs, which will keep them coming back.

Bite-sized chunks

Once you've established this, the best way to manage it, is to break it down into 'bite-sized' chunks. 90 days (a business quarter) tends to be the best timeframe for most business owners. Set it too far ahead and there isn't the daily priority to apply enough time to it. Before you know another quarter has completed and your no further forward. Less than this as we find ourselves under too much pressure to implement as well as manage and we either skip bits or fail to apply diligently enough for that which you have implemented to be fully functional and effective.

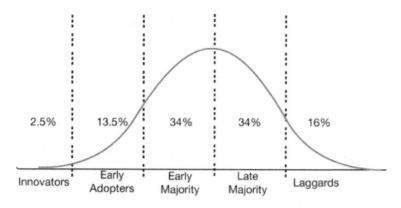

| 2.5% | 13.5% | 34% | 34% | 16% |

| Innovators | Early Adopters | Early Majority | Late Majority | Laggards |

The Business Bell Curve

The bell curve is alive and well. In fact, it is wherever you look.

The bell curve (AKA the normal distribution curve) suggests that in most fields there are some very poor performers and some exceptional performers. These are the two extremes of the curve. In the middle is the rump, where the majority lie.

In most markets, it is fair to say that most businesses look virtually identical. They employ the same sort of people with the same qualifications and backgrounds to use the same software and hardware to sell the same products and services to the same types of customers, using similar websites and similar techniques to sell their similar products at similar prices. It is all so similar.

If you use the bell curve to consider your marketplace, you will find:

- a few dreadful competitors,
- a few stars, the hyper-performers and
- the rump in the middle.

More interesting will be the distribution of profits. The stars will be disproportionately more profitable. Often, the top 20% of performers will account for the top 80% of profits in the marketplace.

Now things start to get interesting. The stars tend to behave in different ways from those in the rump.

Two examples:

EXAMPLE

Blogs

Latent Blogger's tend to blog a couple of times a week. Maybe each blog takes one hour to write and runs to, say, 500 words. As a result, the blog looks like all the other general comment pieces that don't really add a thing of great significance to the already burgeoning body of mediocrity that everyone feels the need to contribute to.

On the other hand, the Early bloggers are very different. They might focus on writing relevant and significant pieces, taking, say, 10 hours to create a 5,000-word piece that people will stop and read because it has depth and breadth and is different from the glorified tweets that most blogs have become.

Prices

Price-takers exist in the Later stages (as opposed to price-makers in the Earlier stages). In the Latent stages, most people feel they are competing on price. In a price-sensitive market, margins get squeezed and it becomes a buyers' market.

Early adopters behave differently. They charge disproportionately higher prices and set themselves apart. As a result, their margins are much higher and they can afford to spend more time and money investing in the brand, the offering, and creating proprietary value-adding products and services.

The same is true of the investments in strategy and planning, product and service design, brand development, training, and development… In fact, I find it difficult to think of a single area where the Early Adopters do not get a disproportionately larger return on their investment…

But does the world really work this way with a nice even distribution between the highs, middles, and lows? Clearly the answer is no.

Research found that performance in 94 percent of these groups did not follow a normal distribution. Rather these groups fall into what is called a "Power Law" distribution.

A *"Power Law"* distribution is sometimes referred to as the *"long tail."* It indicates that people are not "normally distributed" (and the emphasis is on the word normal). In this statistical model there are a small number of people who are "hyper-performers," a broad swathe of people who are "good performers" and a smaller number of people who are "low performers." It essentially accounts for a much wider variation in performance among the sample.

It has very different characteristics from the Bell Curve. In the Power Curve most people fall below the mean (slightly). Roughly 10-15% of the population are above the average (often far above the average), a large population is slightly below average, and a small group are far below average. So, the concept of "average" becomes meaningless. In fact, the implication is that comparison to "average" isn't very useful at all, because

the small number of people who are "hyper-performers" accommodate a very high percentage of the total business value.

Key target area's

One of the biggest challenge's marketers' faces is getting word out to the people who are most likely to become our customers. In fact, the whole goal of all marketing is to "get the right message to the right person at the right time." As marketers we also make sure we can do this at the best price possible.

Here are five steps that will help you better identify who YOUR audience is and HOW you can best connect with them.

Acknowledge that you have a specific target audience

It's important to understand that your products and services have a target audience that can be defined. As a marketer, your primary goal is to find ways to identify who these people are so that you can create marketing campaigns that speak to them directly.

This might sound obvious, but too often marketers assume that what they offer the world has universal appeal and that their target audience is "everybody"! As much as we would all like to believe that it's never true and can get in the way of creating effective marketing campaigns that do talk to the right people.

Determine what criteria you intend to use to identify the consumers you most wish to reach

An audience can be sorted any number of ways based on an almost infinite number of criteria. But your audience is unique to your brands, so you're going to want to identify the factors that can be used to create a better connection between their potential needs and what your company offers.

For starters, are there some demographic points that you can use such as age, gender, or geography to begin to refine who the best recipients are for your products? How about criteria that matches a prospect's beliefs, opinions, attitudes, or intentions with your marketing message?

The goal of this step is to eliminate the people for whom an offer won't be relevant or important. With these people out of the mix, you can now focus your marketing messages to reach the remaining people who are most apt to be interested and willing to take some sort of action when they encounter your marketing message.

Identify what your customers and prospects want most from you.

One of the challenges that most marketers face is that they are too close to their own brands.

While you certainly want to promote your brands and services in a positive light, you also need to be willing to put yourself in the shoes of your target customers as often as possible. Chances are they don't know much (if anything) about your brand or understand the benefits you offer nearly as well as you do. By seeing your brand through new eyes, you can also look for potential weaknesses, areas of potential misuse or misunderstanding, and even things that consumers may object to or find offensive. Taking this step better allows you to create marketing messages and campaigns that fully address possible brand concerns and objections before they occur.

Identify the best channels to use to communicate with these people

What's the best way to reach your target audience? Again, there is no 100 percent right answer on the best channels you can use reach a target audience. For example, a local business looking for a local audience isn't going to need to run a nationwide online search campaign to reach its target audience. Instead, it might rely on an ad in a local directory or even a small local newspaper to get best results.

Start by thinking about how your target audience gets information. What channels do they use? Television? Radio? Newspapers? Webpages? Online search campaigns? You want to make sure that when your target consumers are learning about the world around them that your messages are part of that information stream.

Measure campaign results to determine if you did reach the right people!

Defining your target audience is just the first step. Now, you need to determine if you were correct. It's common for marketers to identify an audience they want to reach only to discover once the campaign starts running that a very different group of people respond to the marketing materials. Again, depending on the types of marketing channels you use, the feedback you will receive can tell you some very important stories.

The bottom line is NOT to assume that just because you have identified an audience and then determined the best criteria to select and reach that audience that your work is done. EVERY campaign you'll run will teach you how to do a better job in the future. However, you need to be open to that feedback and be willing to continually tweak that information to optimize future campaigns resulting in more and more effective results!

3.8 3-5 Year growth plan

Your 3-5 Year Strategic Plan can be viewed as a base camp on the way to the summit. The summit is your BFHAG (or Big Fat Hairy Audacious Goal) which is typically measured 10 to 20 years in the future, which can feel like a lifetime in today's business environment. Your goal here is to set your Targets and identify the Strategic Growth Plans and Scaling Goals you'll need to develop to hit those Targets and move in the direction of achieving your BFHAG.

Typically, you will determine your 3–5-year strategic business plan as part of your Annual Planning session.

Step 1 - Set 3-5Year Growth Targets

Set 3-year targets to define success before you start

Examples of the types of Targets and KPI dashboards you will want to consider include:

1. Revenue
2. Profit (EBITDA)

3.   Revenue/Employee
4.   Market Cap
5.   Cash Flow

You can add or subtract from this list to include the Targets that are most meaningful to your business.

The one Target that should apply for all businesses is Revenue. I challenge you to set a Revenue Target that will allow you to 2,3 even 5X your business over the next 3-5 years.

If you believe you can only grow at a rate of 15% per year, then you will achieve the 2X mark
in 5 years. If you believe you can grow at a rate of 25%, then you will achieve the 2X mark in 3 years. And so on.

Be sure to include the year you will hit those Revenue Targets so that you can hold each other accountable. Strong 3-year strategic plans help you grow revenue and stay competitive and not caught up in the short-term day to day management of your company.

Step 2 - Determine Strategic Winning Moves for Revenue

Think of strategic revenue growth initiatives that can double your top line.

Winning Moves are strategic growth initiatives and actions that enable you to double, Triple even Quadruple your revenue within 3-5 years. These winning moves are often the base camps in the client's quest to reach the summit to achieve their BFHAG (Big Fat Hairy Audacious Goal).

3-5 Year strategic plans do not come from Eureka moments. They are developed over time when you dedicate yourself to designated and uninterrupted think time and should be reviewed every year at your Annual Planning Session.

These 3-year strategic business plans help your company grow and sharpen your competitive advantage. It is this business strategy that sets you apart from the competition.

Step 3 - Determine Strategic Winning Moves for Profit

Determine strategic profit initiatives to increase productivity.

These are the strategic capabilities you'll need to develop to support your growth and reach your 3–5-year Targets. These are usually operational in nature or related to your infrastructure and help you while scaling up.

Some examples of Winning Moves for Profit include the following:

- Leadership & talent growth
- New operating systems
- Opening more locations or a second office
- These will be very specific to your company's needs.

You cannot grow your business by cutting costs. It is important to have clear Winning Moves to better focus your team on revenue growth to help grow the top line.

Winning Moves are your company's leading indicator of future revenue growth and financial health. Conversely, lack of Winning Moves is the leading indicator that you will hit the growth ceiling and stall. You cannot cut costs to get growth.

Step 4: Four Step Process to Determine Your Winning Moves for Revenue

Choose the right strategic growth initiatives with our template to get you started

Brainstorm Winning Moves

Start by brainstorming a comprehensive list of at least 20 potential ways your team can think of to increase revenue. Some ideas to jump-start the revenue brainstorming process are the following:

- What's my competition not willing to do?
- What do our customers hate but must put up with?
- Do I have an asset or diamond in my backyard?
- What's the biggest barrier to entry for my prospects and how can I remove it?
- Are there opportunities to consider through partnership, acquisition, or joint venture?
- What are some big ideas or opportunities we have discussed in the past, but not acted on?

Vote on the Top 5-8

Have the team consider each idea and vote on the top three they recommend investing time and energy in considering. Choose the top 5-8 ideas with the most votes.

Evaluate & Rank Top 5-8 Ideas

Evaluate and rank each of the top 5-8 ideas based on two scales, Revenue Impact, and Ease.

Revenue Impact - On a scale of 1-10, what is the potential impact this move could have on revenue? A score of 10 would indicate that this move alone could more than double your current revenue.

Easy to do - On a scale of 1-10, how easy would it be to get this done? A score of 10 would indicate that it would be very easy to execute because you already have all the expertise and resources necessary, and it's synergistic with your other activities.

Choose Your 1-3 Winning Moves

Select the few Winning Moves you want to include in your 3–5-year plan. Decide what to say yes to and what to say no to. Classify each idea:

- Winning Move for Revenue= part of 3–5-year plan; revenue growth
- Winning Move for Profit= part of 3–5-year plan; infrastructure, scalability, and efficiency,
- Idea Bench = Later, other Moves are more important
- Dead = Stop, losing move

These are the steps to identify the 1-3 Winning Moves you want to include in your 3–5-year plan. Now you're ready to begin the process of developing and implementing them. You may be interested in our blog post that includes a SlideShare to help you get started to develop Winning Moves to double your revenue.

Five Steps to Advance Your Winning Moves
How to execute your strategic initiatives to achieve your goals

1. Name Your Strategic Winning Moves

Name each winning move idea uniquely to communicate the idea clearly with your team. Naming your winning move should intensify team focus and sell the idea internally and externally.

2. Find the "Who"

The right "who" can accelerate your progress. Ask these questions to find the "who":

- Who has the most experience and expertise for this Winning Move?
- Do we have the resources or need help?
- How does this impact cost, hiring, etc.?

3.   Develop the 3-5 Year Revenue Growth Projections

Winning Moves must bring you revenue growth. What is your projection for the next three to five years?

4.   Identify & Test Your Assumptions

Identify the assumptions leading you to believe the Revenue Impact and Ease rankings are accurate. Have the team document up to 5 assumptions they are making on each idea, then allow time to use data and experience to test those assumptions. This process aids to develop Winning Moves based on facts instead of emotion.

Ask these questions before jumping in to execute your 3–5-year strategic growth initiative:

- What are my top 5 assumptions on why this move will work?
- What are the key obstacles to overcome?
- What deal breakers must we validate before jumping in?
- Are there any government policies and regulations to consider?
- What trends are we relying on for success?

5.   Adjust and Test Again

Record the change or adjustment to make based on the real-world insights and learnings. As you begin to put these Winning Moves into action, it's important that you keep testing your assumptions, documenting learnings, and adjusting the plan as you go along. Visit our blog with 16 strategic planning tips to keep your strategic plan alive during the year.

If your industry is growing faster than 25% per year, you will need to set a more aggressive Revenue Target. You never want to grow slower than your industry or you will be losing market share to your competition. If this is the case, you will need to set a target that is more than 2X your current revenue in 3 years.

3.9 Identifying Requirements

Identified Value Proposition, Brand, Investment requirements

The two skills needed to leverage the power of a value proposition:

1. You need to be able to identify an effective value proposition.
2. You need to be able to express an effective value proposition.

Identify your value proposition

Characteristics of an effective value proposition:

1. Value proposition is the primary reason a prospect should buy from you.
2. This requires you to differentiate your offer from competitors.
3. You may match a competitor on every dimension of value except one.
4. In at least one element of value, you need to excel.
5. In this way you become the best choice for your optimum customer.

There is a difference between the value proposition for your company and for your product. You must address both.

Use a 1-5 scale to rate the quality and uniqueness of your value proposition:

1. Limited value to a small market. Extensive competition and/or few barriers to entry.
2. Substantial value to a medium-sized market. Limited competition and/or significant barriers to entry.
3. Product or service with strong product differentiation, but little competitive protection.
4. Unique product or service that is highly valuable to a large market, and strong competitive protection and/or extensive barriers to entry. This may take the form of a registered patent or limited access to product components.
5. Unique product or service that is highly valuable to a large market, and exclusive or near exclusive control of essential product components. May include a registered patent.

If your value proposition does not rank as a 3 or better on this scale, you should take a critical look at your core business.

Express your value proposition

Principles for expressing a value proposition effectively:

1. Ask yourself: "Why should my ideal prospect (the group you intend to serve) buy from me instead of a competitor?"
2. Compare your answer with the claims of your main competitors.
3. Refine your value proposition until you can articulate it in a single, instantly credible, sentence.

4. If you had just 10 words with which to describe why people should buy from your company instead of someone else, what would you communicate?

Brand

Branding is a way of defining your business to yourself, your team, and your external audiences. It could be called the business' 'identity', but only on the understanding that it embodies the core of what the business is and its values, not just what it looks and sounds like. Customers of all sorts of businesses are so savvy today that they can see through most attempts by companies to gloss, spin or charm their way to sales.

The benefits that a strategically defined brand can bring are the same as when people fall in love with each other. When customers connect emotively - because they share the same values and beliefs as the brand - it leads to higher sales and better brand differentiation.

A strong brand encourages loyalty, advocacy. It can even protect your price in times when competitors rely on promotional discounts to drive sales. Your brand can also give you the ideal platform from which to extend your offering or range.

3.10 Preparing for Investment

The answer largely depends on your understanding of how fundraising should be done.

There are 3 Common fundraising mistakes to avoid. Sadly, the dos and don'ts of fundraising are poorly understood by many business owners.

1. **Do not base your fundraising strategies on other people's success stories**

It doesn't matter if you read it in a book or heard it down the pub, a success story is like every other story: there will be embellishments and/or missing details. But crucially, someone else's route to glory isn't always the path best suited to you, your team, or your product.

2. Do not treat fundraising as a part-time job

Regardless of the size and scale, fund raising should be treated as a full-time project. It is far too important to have anything but your full attention.

3. Do not think fundraising is a solo effort

Get your team involved. Investors like to see the people they will be backing, and that's not just you. With your team at the first meeting, a potential funder's questions can be answered there and then. There's no long-winded

follow-up process that risks your potential investor losing interest or investing their money with a more efficient operation.

Perseverance and planning are crucial

"I'm convinced that about half of what separates the successful entrepreneurs from the non-successful ones is pure perseverance."

Steve Jobs

Wise words, but there's another important P-word: planning. And the first thing you need to do when putting together your fundraising plan is to make a decision about debt.

5 Steps to Investor Success

Taking your business to the next level is hard. As you are preparing for investment, a million questions jump to mind.

- Is now the right time to ask for investment?
- What options do I have?
- How much should I ask for?
- Am I ready?

Take the guesswork out of it with this thorough checklist that walks you through everything you'll need to secure funding.

1. **The investment proposition: Why should anyone invest in you?**

Just having a good idea won't do. You'll need sensible milestones, a strong value proposition and a thorough knowledge of your investors to secure that first meeting.

- Do you know who you're pitching to?
  There are a million options out there, so you should know whether venture capitalists, angels, or crowdfunding are the right fit. Each provides a different level of involvement in the business and have different expectations. Some will only cater to certain sectors or have similar products in their portfolios already.

  Start off with a list of about 30 investors, looking out for those with a proven track record in your industry, and get their contact information. Some will receive more than 250 proposals a month, so make that first communication count.
- What is your value proposition?
  It all starts with an elevator pitch. You should be able to describe what your company does in a simple sentence, as well as what value it brings to the market.
- What problem are you solving?

You need to clearly convey the actual pain point that you're addressing and how that problem affects your potential customer base.

- How well do you know your target market?
  Investors will want to know how big the market is, and that you have a realistic plan to conquer a segment of that market.
- Have you prepared a compelling teaser proposal for potential investors?
  That initial email is an opportunity to let investors have a brief overview of your investment opportunity. Outline who you are, the problem your business solves, and provide information about the market, and what you need funding for. Be sure to keep the focus on the investment opportunity, not the business.

2. The pitch deck

Once you've made it through to the first meeting, you need to wow them with your presentation. Investors are fuelled by the fear of missing the next unicorn, but they also fear losing money. To get them over the hump, make sure your numbers are on point.

While your pitch presentation should reiterate your vision, value proposition, and opportunity, focus on providing data-centric information on your business and revenue streams.

- **Have you prepared a revenue model?**
  Go over your business plan and how you intend to turn a profit. Identify your potential clients and revenue streams, as well as where you fit in the competitive landscape. Break down revenue projections for at least the next 12 months, but preferably 3 years.
- **Can you provide updated financial projections?**

Investors will conduct due diligence and expect your pitch deck to include a summary of your financials. Be prepared to go through your cash needs.

Can you demonstrate traction?

Early-stage companies will not always be able to show a lot of metrics proving adoption, but any sales or early adopter data will help. It's paramount to prove that you have a keen understanding of both engagement and operational metrics, and how they validate your concept.

Have you put together a marketing strategy?

Make sure that you can churn out a clear funnel and/or go-to-market strategy, whatever the case may be. Know your customer acquisition costs and lifetime values.

What does your product roadmap look like?

Investors need to know that you have a plan and won't squander their funds. Outline the steps you've taken so far, your major goals and the milestones you're setting up to hit in the next 18 months, down to features and costs.

Does your presentation get to the point?

All your pitch deck needs are a small number of slides, each sending one message. They should focus on your product, market, business model, traction, financial projections, team, competitors, exit strategy and above all your investment proposition. When in doubt, use Guy Kawasaki's 10/20/30 rule: Keep it under 10 slides, talk for no more than 20 minutes, and use a font size no bigger than 30.

3. Justifiable valuation

The value you put on your company will determine how many shares you're letting go of, so it should be defensible.

⊙ **Do you have a valuation?**
Putting your valuation together can be daunting. You're dealing with current annualised revenues, cash investments, scalability, and monthly profitability, among others. Don't worry, we've created a guide and a valuation scorecard to get you going.

⊙ **Is it realistic?**
Being able to defend your valuation is crucial, so make sure you have a range that fits your expectations and can back it up with industry-specific benchmarks.⊡Research companies like yours in terms of stage and sector to benchmark your valuation.

⊙ **Have you thought about the future?**
If this is your first raise, rest assured that it will not be your last. If your valuation is high now, it will affect future valuations and therefore your ability to raise capital in series A and beyond.

⊙ **Have you factored in the broader market context?**
Economic uncertainty has become a norm for the UK since 2016; the impact of Covid-19 has exacerbated that. Investors are being ultra-cautious in this environment, so take that into account when setting a valuation.

4. Team

Proven management and a diverse team are critical to attaining funding. Investors want to know your plans are backed by a team that can deliver. At the end of the day, people invest in people.

◎ **What is your team's skill set?**

The more diverse your team's skills, the better. You want to create a team made up of people with expertise in marketing & sales, finance, and product development.

◎ **Does the management team have a proven track record?**

The people behind the scenes should be motivated and committed to the company full-time. However passionate they are, though, investors favour teams that have grown/exited a business before.

5. Exit Strategy

How will investors make their money back? Will it be through a trade sale or an IPO? Make sure you have credible answers to these questions.

◎ **Have you considered your exit strategy?**

Look at similar company exits, weigh the benefits of IPO versus sale, and be clear on what your eventual aim is.

◎ **Are the founders aligned on the exit strategy?**

Investors will want to know if there are any major disagreements amongst founders, and alignment on an exit strategy is as major as it gets. Make sure everyone is on the same page before investor meetings.

Securing funding is not for the faint of heart, and one mistake could make or break you.

In fact, studies show that most pitches get thrown out because of market issues, management profiles, and, finally, financials.

Doing it can be the springboard to the 'next level' in business. But it's a strategy not a punt, it needs work, effort, time, consideration, and funding!

However, the first thing you need to do when putting together your fundraising plan is to make a decision about debt.

You see, there's bad debt and good debt. But you must determine how you feel about either!

Bad debt is borrowing because you must! It's too easy to access, and yet always expensive and risky, and should be avoided wherever possible.

Meanwhile, there's also good debt!

Good debt is borrowing because you choose to, can and is part of a strategic plan. And whilst it's more difficult to secure, it's far cheaper (than bad debt) and can accelerate the business far quicker than organic growth.

5 Ways to unlock finance for your business

1.   Identify whether you need equity, debt, or both

Many people automatically start thinking about raising all the money they need as equity, failing to consider the consequences regarding dilution. Opting to go this route can also result in poor decisions, such as raising the amount of money that doesn't impact the entrepreneur's shareholding, rather than raising the amount that is required.

Incredibly, the debt option is often forgotten. So long as there I the right management with the right track record, there are plenty of debt providers willing to assist early-stage businesses (although this will not be the traditional banks). Many

business owners fail to fully appreciate that the debt route can be the superior option: in addition to not affecting equity, it can be a quicker and easier source of funds, which allows the business owner a speedier return to running a business. However, a combination of debt and equity is often the ideal solution. This enables a cheaper cost of capital for the company: debt is entitled to interest rather than a dividend.

The balance of debt and equity is important, with 30% equity and 70% debt being a good ratio; this is a ratio that tax authorities and capital providers like to see. This ratio also makes the company more likely to attract further equity investment, as potential shareholders can see that the management understands the advantages of debt being part

of a company's financing strategy. With the equity/debt aspect of your plan in place, it's time for spreadsheets.

2. Create a strong financial model

With your figures entered in a spreadsheet, or dedicated planning software, test them. Run several likely scenarios; these can be shown to potential equity investors and debt providers, demonstrating that you are prepared for different outcomes.

Remember, these must show the different types of returns from the different sources of capital. And you will need to produce a cashflow forecast for at least the next 12-18 months. You'll be able to impress by working out any dependencies and talking through how these will be managed.

3. Be realistic about your valuation

For a credible idea of the value of your company, compare the most recent valuations for transactions in your area. Don't be swayed by outlier valuations; look to the middle ground. Potential investors are familiar with the idea of something being too good to be true. With all the information you will need pulled together, the next stage is to work on how that information will be presented.

4. Prepare a one-page summary of the opportunity

This is the correct format for initial contacts. If your proposition can't be summarised in one page, you're not ready to speak to potential investors, the majority of whom prefer a summary. If they're interested, they'll ask for more detail.

This one-page document should include:

- A summary of the opportunity
- The amount of investment being sought
- The kind of business going to be generated; and
- The potential return.
- Be clear, be concise.

When a potential investor asks for more information, you need to compile a document that does this on its own. If it needs you to be in the room explaining it, it's no good.

It needs to answer the following questions:

- What is the business?
- Who are the management team?
- What is the market size?
- What is the opportunity within the market?
- How much money is needed?
- What is the money going to be spent on?
- What kind of business will be created post investment?

Have this document ready before you send out the one-page summary; you don't want to put off a potential investor by delaying sending the follow up document, or by that document being sub-standard because it was rushed.

- How to choose the right business loan
- How to maximise your chances of securing a small business loan
- What to do when the bank says 'No'

5. **Where do you look for the money?**

    Who you approach largely depends on the scale of your
    ambition. There are people who write £100 million cheques
    (although they're not the easiest people to get in front of), and
    there are EIS/SEIS funds, VCT funds, and plenty of pools of EIS
    investors if your fundraising falls into the £1-5 million range.

    If the funds you're looking for are less than that, there are
    Angel Investors, although there is often an up-front fee for
    being introduced, so be sure the Angels are right for your
    sector. It's important not to discount your own connections,
    including family and friends. These can be the best investors
    and debt providers.

6. **When contacting investors, preparation is key**

    Target your funders carefully. Background research will
    prevent you from wasting valuable time and energy chasing
    people who would never invest in your area, or your size of
    business, or your geographical location, or your target
    customers, etc.

    These steps can't guarantee you'll raise the funds you need –
    fundraising can be more art than science – but preparation,
    putting in the necessary time, and perseverance all increase
    the likelihood of success.

Investment opportunities identified

5 Things Investors Want to Know Before Signing a Cheque

Pitching your idea to investors, regardless of if they are
bankers, VCs, or angels, can be intimidating, so prepare by
putting yourself in the investor's shoes. What do they look for
when evaluating your company? Here is a list of the five most

important things that an investor wants to know before sinking money in a company.

1. Financial performance

You need to know your numbers. Prove to potential investors that your company has excellent financial performance, especially if you are seeking funding from a bank. Venture capitalists will look for a potential of high returns and a clear exit opportunity.

Prepare to answer questions about the financial stability of your company. Investors will ask if your company shows signs of growth and if you have plans such as issuing shares or borrowing money to stimulate growth.

Your debt repayment plan should also be properly presented. Prove your business can handle its financial obligations.

When pitching to investors based on your company's financial performance, it's advisable to show proof that your current assets are enough to cover current or short-term liabilities. Expect investors to evaluate your revenue streams, acquisition cost and turnover rates.

2. Background and experience in the industry

Investors don't want entrepreneurs to make mistakes on their dime. Investors look for experienced entrepreneurs and management teams with a track record of high performance and leadership in the company's industry or in prior ventures. Most investors will research your business experience and your background in the industry. Passion and commitment should be evident to inspire confidence in investors and stakeholders.

"Investor fit" is particularly important to angel investors compared to venture capital fund managers. Angel investors place great importance on "chemistry" between themselves and the entrepreneur because they generally take a more hands-on approach in the businesses, they invest in.

Tim Ferriss, an entrepreneur, and angel investor has mentioned that he looks for founders who have ideally done something high stress when failure or rejection is constant on a small or large scale almost every day.

3. **Company uniqueness**

   Your product or services need to be unique. Prove to your investors, with concrete evidence, that your market potential is big enough to make investing worthwhile.

   Venture capitalists are influenced by product characteristics such as proprietary features and competitive advantage.

   Investors look for features that distinguish you from potential competitors and give you some sort of advantage, such as intellectual property protection, exclusive licenses and exclusive marketing and distribution relationships.

4. **Effective business model**

   Your company will start to display its strategic value as soon as it begins to generate profits. Present the business model that you are currently using and prove that it will help your company become more profitable.

   Different types of investors seek different attributes from a business plan. It's important to customize your business plan and pitch to each investor. For example, venture capital fund managers and angel investors tend to put more emphasis on both market and finance issues, so those are areas that you should focus on when approaching these types of investors.

5. **Large market size**

   Angel investors typically invest in solutions that address major problems for significantly large target markets. On the other hand, venture capitalists look at market characteristics such as significant growth and limited competition when investing.

   The larger and more stable customer base that your brand has, the stronger competitive advantage you will have when pitching to investors. A larger and more stable customer base will serve as proof that your company has a great impact to its target market.

   Investors look for companies that can grow quickly and manage this high growth scale. Investors must see that the company can generate significant profits beyond the initial product idea with adequate financial projections and a plan to include multiple sources of revenue.

3.11 Diary Blocking

Diary blocking to work ON the business (50%)

As any professional will know, time is a valuable commodity, and it must be managed wisely. For investors and busy entrepreneurs however, this is particularly important. Often, entrepreneurs are required to work on numerous tasks or projects at once and this can result in demanding schedules and time-sensitive conflicts.

Dealing with investors, media, and clients, as well as running the business and taking on new staff can leave entrepreneurs with very little free time. Whilst an existing company may have the resources to hire additional in-house personnel, building a business can be the busiest time for entrepreneurs.

Due to this, it's essential that diaries are managed properly. Entrepreneurs who are struggling to find enough hours in the day may notice that a few key changes to their diary management releases a significant amount of time.

1. **Plan your diary in advance**

    Last-minute meetings or urgent calls will always crop up but planning your diary in advance will ensure that everything else is scheduled. Although you'll need to add events to your calendar daily, taking a few minutes to plan your diary at the start of each week can help you to visualise what the next seven days will entail. Following this, you can schedule additional meetings, conferences or calls at times which are appropriate for you.

2. **Take advantage of colour codes .**

    Most professionals rely on electronic or online diary management, and this offers many advantages. Easy to update and accessible from anywhere, online calendars ensure that you can always check what's coming up.

    However, it's important to get the most out of diary management software and there's bound to be numerous features you're not using. Colour coding your engagements can be an extremely useful way to organise your diary. Highlighting different types of engagements in varying colours means that you can see what events are approaching, just by glancing at your diary. Meetings with potential investors, conferences with in-house colleagues and even important

    family events can be categorised so that you're able to recognise them instantly, rather than having to read through your daily list of appointments.

3. **Factor in breaks**

   Unfortunately, entrepreneurs often find it hard to switch off and don't usually take as many breaks as they should.

   Over time, this can have a negative effect on their professional lives, as well as their health and well-being. When managing your diary, it's vital to include regular breaks and time away from the office. In addition to factoring a daily lunch break into your diary, for example, you may need to include specific days off.

   Whilst most people work at least five days per week, busy entrepreneurs often end up working more than this. When launching a business, working over the weekends, early in the morning and late into the evening isn't uncommon. Although your business may require such input at the start, it's crucial that you schedule regular breaks so that you don't suffer from the strain of overwork.

4. **Collate as many details as possible**

   When adding something to your diary, don't be tempted to simply note down vague details. Whilst you might have additional information stored in your head, it can be difficult to recall it later.

   For example, rather than simply diarising a meeting with specific person, you'll need to make a note of where the meeting is to be held; the topic (including any preparation that might be required); any other attendees; the nature of the meeting and the contact details of the host. Whilst you may have the information elsewhere, adding these details to your diary means that you can access it quickly and easily, should you need to.

5. Use your time wisely

When you're arranging events or diarising meetings, it's vital to be aware of other engagements.

For example, if you are arranging two out-of-office meetings you may want to schedule them on the same day, at nearby locations.

This can cut down on your travel time and ensure that you aren't left idle between events.

Similarly, determine whether face-to-face meetings can be changed to phone calls, or even video conferencing. Often this cuts down on the time a discussion takes but still enables you to achieve the same results.

6. Back-up your diary

Once you implement all your diary management skills, you'll realise just how useful your diary is. In fact, most entrepreneurs and professionals would struggle to operate without a properly managed diary. It's vital, therefore, that your calendar is properly backed up, in case there is an electronic or internet issue. Unfortunately, this can happen all too frequently, and you risk losing anything you haven't secured.

Having a data recovery plan and keeping your diary backed up via cloud computing, for example, ensures that you can access the document from wherever you are and that you aren't solely reliant on hardware. If a hard drive or server fails, it could delete crucial data, but if it's also stored virtually, you'll be able to access a back-up instantaneously.

7. Get professional help with diary management

Organising a diary is no easy feat, particularly for a busy entrepreneur. Whilst it may be tempting to overlook the management of your calendar when you have so many other tasks to do, but this can result in you missing important events, being ill-prepared and losing crucial time.

I now ensure 40% of my working week is BLOCKED and allocated for me to work ON the business! No, I'm not yet (and possibly don't really want to be) at a stage where ALL my time is blocked out to working ON the business! I really enjoy what I do and will probably recruit an MD ahead of becoming the chairman so far removed from the element of the business I most enjoy. However, it is crucial to spend ALLOCATED time EVERY week working ON both YOU and YOUR business. This might be switching your phone off and taking a walk along the beach or through a wood! You'd be AMAZED as to how productive simply going for a walk can be to clear your head and begin to uncomplicate things!

3.12 Business model Generation

Creating a business model isn't simply about completing your business plan or determining which products to pursue. It's about mapping out how you will create ongoing value for your customers.

Where will your business idea start, how should it progress, and when will you know you've been successful? How will you create value for customers? Follow these simple steps to securing a strong business model.

1. **Identify your specific audience**

   Targeting a wide audience won't allow your business to home in on customers who truly need and want your product or service. Instead, when creating your business model, narrow your audience down to two or three detailed buyer personas. Outline each persona's demographics, common challenges and the solutions your company will offer. As an example, Home Depot might appeal to everyone or carry a product the average person needs, but the company's primary target market is homeowners and builders.

2. **Establish business processes.**

   Before your business can go live, you need to understand the activities required to make your business model work. Determine key business activities by first identifying the core aspect of your business's offering. Are you responsible for providing a service, shipping a product, or offering consulting? In the case of Ticketbis, an online ticket exchange marketplace, key business processes include marketing and product delivery management.

3. **Record key business resources.**

   What does your company need to carry out daily processes, find new customers and reach business goals? Document essential business resources to ensure your business model is adequately prepared to sustain the needs of your business. Common resource examples may include a website, capital, warehouses, intellectual property, and customer lists.

4. **Develop a strong value proposition.**
   How will your company stand out among the competition? Do you provide an innovative service, revolutionary product, or a new twist on an old favourite? Establishing exactly what your

business offers and why it's better than competitors is the beginning of a strong value proposition. Once you've got a few value propositions defined, link each one to a service or product delivery system to determine how you will remain valuable to customers over time.

5. **Determine key business partners.**

   No business can function properly (let alone reach established goals) without key partners that contribute to the business's ability to serve customers. When creating a business model, select key partners, like suppliers, strategic alliances, or advertising partners. Using the previous example of Home Depot, key business partners may be lumber suppliers, parts wholesalers, and logistics companies.

6. **Create a demand generation strategy.**

   Unless you're taking a radical approach to launching your company, you'll need a strategy that builds interest in your business, generates leads, and is designed to close sales. How will customers find you? More importantly, what should they do once they become aware of your brand? Developing a

   demand generation strategy creates a blueprint of the customer's journey while documenting the key motivators for acting.

7. **Leave room for innovation.**

   When launching a company and developing a business model, your business plan is based on many assumptions. After all, until you begin to welcome paying customers, you don't truly know if your business model will meet their ongoing needs.

   For this reason, it's important to leave room for future innovations. Don't make a critical mistake by thinking your initial plan is a static document. Instead, review it often and implement changes as needed.

3.13 ON not IN

I regard Michael Gerber as one of the For-fathers of Modern Entrepreneurship. He has helped transform 70,000-plus businesses in 145 countries over the past 25 years. His New York Times best-selling book, The E-Myth Revisited, has sold more than five million copies, and continues to be a regular purchase for many SME business owners.

Within the book he shares one of the biggest bottlenecks in many businesses is that owners of businesses remain the operator within their business, and not the business owner.

He defines the two as an operator is someone who builds their business around them. And even when they take on staff, they employ them in supportive roles that keep them as the primary fee earner within the business.

Whereas, a business owner sees the risk of doing this, and quickly works to build a team of those they can allocate work to, with whom they can then support, coach, mentor whilst continuing to generate the enquiries and growing the business.

3.14 Leverage models

Work on your greater vision and you'll find a way to succeed.

By applying the power of leverage to business, you can (with less effort) accomplish a lot more. Without it, you increase your risk of burnout and frustration, and limit your rewards.

Put simply, leverage is all about multiplying gains and making money work for you. In this challenging new economy, you need every advantage you can get, especially in entrepreneurship and business. Gaining the competitive advantage isn't easy. Chaos is almost guaranteed, but the upside outweighs the tough times. Here are six fail-proof ways to give yourself the ultimate leverage.

1. **Position Rather Than Prospect**

Everybody is looking for prospects, clients, and customers. This never-ending search process will eventually burn you out and is tough to scale on a consistent basis. An easier way to approach your business is to position yourself as the leading authority — the expert, specialist, or the trusted advisor — on your subject. This takes very strategic and intentional action, but the rewards are exponential.

When you're perceived as the expert, people will start coming to you. Be more elite and exclusive. Define what makes your business different. Once you figure out what makes you unique, get more attention. Start leveraging your experience through other people's proven platforms. Whom could you connect with that already has influence and impact within your target market? Some examples include publications, podcasts, features, magazines, speaking events and sponsorship opportunities. You will expand your reach a lot faster.

2. **Know That Plans Fail, But Movements Don't**

Reposition your business and make it about something. Think about Disney; it's not about movies or about amusement parks or about cruises — it's about being part of a brand where dreams come true. Or think about how Subway went from being a fast-food chain to a weight-loss program. Most companies, whether start-ups or billion-pound corporations, don't have compelling stories or visions behind them. The entrepreneurs on a mission bigger than themselves are always attract top-tier talent. Life becomes much more fulfilling when you're involved in a movement or a cause greater than yourself.

3. Stand on the Shoulders of Giants

You don't need to reinvent the wheel, and you certainly don't need to figure everything out yourself. Find something that is already working and make it better or find your niche and do what the best are already doing. In an interview with Gary Vaynerchuk, he said, *"A penguin cannot become a giraffe. So just be the best penguin you can be."*

A smart person learns from their mistakes. Those wanting world-class results learn from other peoples' mistakes so they can shorten their learning curve. Nothing will make a bigger impact on your future than the people you associate with daily.

4. Become a People Developer

You not only need a solid team around you, but you need to know how to develop and lead that team. When you watch sports, you'll find the most successful teams are the ones that play very well together. They complement each other, and they all have one single focus: winning.

The same goes for business and life. The people you have in your inner circle is your team. Who needs to be on that team to make sure it's a "dream team?"

5. Create Raving Fans and Advocates

Business is the management of promises, and if you can consistently deliver and exceed the promises you make to all your customers, you're ahead of the game. It's much more expensive to get a new customer than it is to take care of the ones you already have.

The purpose of business is to create raving fans and advocates who will go out of their way to promote what you do — not because you asked them, but because they want to. Every person in your organization should be responsible for outstanding client support and service, from the reception to the mail room to the CEO. You must create a culture where people are passionate about meeting clients' needs.

6. **Work on the Business, Not Just in the Business**

Most people get so caught up in the day-to-day grind of making everything work properly that they forget about working on the vision. So, every week, work on your strategy for the year and where you want to be a year from now. Plan your long-term strategies before you plan your tactics: where you plan to go, who you want to be, and what types of clients you want to attract.

3.15 Pitch Perfect

How to Prepare to Pitch Investors

There are a few things you can do to prepare to pitch investors that will help you out when you're actually in the room.

1. Understand What Different Investors Need

Though there are several kinds of investors, by far the two most common are venture capitalists (VCs) and angel investors.

The way you prepare your pitch will differ slightly depending on whether you're speaking to a VC or an angel.

How To Pitch Venture Capitalists
VCs are more thorough, detail-oriented, and are interested in the numbers.

They are writing checks on behalf of a group of investors, so they have strong obligations to make smart decisions.

When pitching VCs, focus on details, metrics, and potential risks.

How To Pitch Angel Investors
Angel investors are high net worth individuals, meaning they are operating as sole investors.

This means that, in general, angels are quicker to act. When pitching to angel investors, focus more on the big picture, the potential upside, and the huge market your product addresses.

2. Prepare for The Appropriate Amount of Time
Most investors take meetings in slots, meaning you'll know how much time you'll need to fill.

This will usually be 10-20 minutes, though it can be longer.

If you've only got 10 minutes, for example, your pitch is going to look very different to if you have 30.

Don't forget to prepare for Q&A time, which will typically be allotted also (for example you might have a 30-minute meeting with 20 minutes to pitch and 10 minutes for questions, or vice versa).

Practice handling improvised Q&A by conducting practice pitches to friends, family, or others who are unfamiliar with your start-up.

3. Do Your Homework on Each Investor
Don't make the mistake of assuming every investor is interested in the same details.

Do your research on each investor you're about to meet, and try to uncover details such as:

- Start-ups they've invested in before
- What makes them say yes (and no)
- The kinds of questions they ask

You might not be able to find all of this info in a simple Google search, but a couple of phone calls to founders who've dealt with that investor before can be a great place to start.

4. Don't Start with Your Ideal Investor
It's a pretty rare occurrence to completely nail your first pitch and secure a deal right then and there.

More likely, you'll hear 'no' from several investors before you finally secure funding.

The mindset to have here is that from each interaction with an investor, each no you receive, you learn something.

You'll learn something about how to pitch your company, how to answer common questions, and about the kinds of information investors expect from you.

With this in mind, it can often be wise not to start with your ideal investor.

By meeting 4 or 5 other investors first, you'll refine your pitch and story, and be much better prepared when you do meet the investor you most want to work with.

What To Cover During Your Investor Pitch

1. Start with Your Elevator Pitch
The last thing you want is an investor who has no idea where you're headed with your pitch.

So, the first thing you want to do when pitching an investor is start with your elevator pitch. This is like a summary of the whole pitch you're about to give, wrapped up in about 30 seconds.

Your elevator pitch should describe:

- What the problem is
- What your solution is
- What your core value prop is

Starting here ensures the investor is on the same playing field as you, as you move into the next stage.

Identify Market Problem

2. Tell A Compelling Story

Most founders find this step fairly easy, as they often have a compelling story to tell.

Think: What was the problem you noticed that made you go *"Hey, someone needs to fix this, and that someone is me!"?*

That's the story you want to tell.

The idea here is that you're:

- Calling out a specific audience (the group your product helps)
- Identifying a common problem
- Describing the emotional reaction they have to that pain point

3. Don't leave out the Details

As exciting as this big story is, however, investors don't just dole out cash for big dreams.

They need details, projections, and numbers.

Use data throughout your pitch presentation to underpin the statements you're making.

For example, when discussing future growth plans, you should provide financial projections based on several likely scenarios.

4. Be clear on how much investment you need, and how you'll use it

Here's what investors don't want to hear:

"We'll take as much as you can give us."

All that says to the investor you're pitching is *"We don't know how much we need to build this company"*.

Instead, you want to tell investors exactly how much funding you require.

Here, describe:

- How much funding you're seeking
- How long you expect that to last (your runway)
- What you're going to use the funding for (marketing, product development, etc)
- Where you'll be when the money runs out (e.g. are you aiming to achieve profitability or to get to a point where you'd be eligible for the next funding round).

5. Go Big on the Market Potential

When discussing the market that your solution addresses, you need to go big.

Ask yourself this question:
Considering all possible current and future uses of this product, what is the size of our total addressable market?

Investors are rarely motivated by small numbers, so be sure to go large with this.

Of course, this needs to be balanced with a hearty dose of realism.

Savvy investors know pumped-up numbers when they see them, meaning any claims you make regarding market potential (or any financial projections for that matter), should be grounded in sound figures.

That is, you should be prepared to demonstrate how you've arrived at those estimates and be able to explain your math with precision.

6. Accurately describe the Competitive Landscape
Products rarely exist in a vacuum without some form of competition.

Even if you are first to market with a specific feature or product vision, you'll still be competing for share of wallet in your sector, and with other start-ups who may have similar products in development.

Be sure to do your research here, and present a thorough analysis of your industry and competitors, including their strengths and weaknesses.

7. Discuss potential risks to your Business
No business venture is risk-free. Unfortunately, many founders are so optimistic about their concept that they forget to consider the possibility of external risk.

Examples to include in your investor pitch include:

- Legal risks
- Technological risks
- Regulatory risks
- Political risks
- Liability risks

Be prepared to answer questions about how you plan to approach and mitigate each of these risks as well.

8. Outline your Marketing Strategy

How do you plan to take your product to market? How are people going to find out about you? And how do you plan to attract new customers?

We all love exciting new ideas, but investors know that the old "build it and they will come" trope simply doesn't hold true.

In your pitch, you'll need to describe to potential investors your strategy for marketing your brand, whether that be through trade shows, content marketing, a large Product Hunt launch, or through direct sales.

9. Describe Your Revenue Model

Your revenue model describes how you'll monetize your offering.

This includes:

- Different plans/tiers
- Whether you're charging a monthly, annual, or one-off fee
- Initial pricing points

A good pitch also includes a simple breakdown of how this model relates to total annual revenue goals.

10. Include a demo if possible

If you already have a prototype or MVP version of your product, then providing a demonstration during your investor pitch is crucial.

This provides tangible evidence of how the product works, what the user experience is like, and gets potential investors to actually engage with your vision.

11. Talk up your Team

Investors want to know that you've got three things right:

- The right idea (suitably solving a common problem)
- The right timing (a large addressable market)
- The right team (the appropriate people to deliver the vision)

During your pitch, include a section on your current team, and describe your expertise, experience, and credentials, as relevant to your company.

This will help give investors confidence in your ability to see bring the concept to market, and can also give them an indication as to areas where you'll need further assistance (which they may be able to help provide).

12. Cover your Exit Strategy

In early funding stages (such as seed funding rounds), investors may be less interested in knowing about your exit strategy.

As you progress as a company, however, and investment amounts climb into the millions, this becomes a crucial question for angels and VCs alike.

- Is your plan to go public?
- To get acquired?
- Management buyout?

State your desired method, and provide some context for your exit strategy.

13. Don't evade tough Questions

Appointments to pitch investors almost always include some time for questions and answers.

Though you've prepared as best you can, you can never know exactly what your investors are going to ask (otherwise you probably would have included that information in your pitch).

When you do get thrown a curveball, however, try to avoid answers like *"I don't know"* or *"I'll cover that later in the presentation"*.

Look, it's okay not to know the answer to a question, and we're certainly not saying you should fabricate answers.

But you should understand that when investors are asking hard questions, it means they're engaged, and they're at least somewhat interested.

They may even be testing your ability to think on your feet.

So, when you're asked a difficult question, do your best to provide an answer, but do so with humility and be honest about the fact that you're not as well prepared for that question as you should be.

For example *"As far as I know, [answer], but that's something I should know the answer to so thank you for bringing it up. Let me come back to you after this meeting to confirm that's correct."*

14. Always follow up with a Thank You note
After every pitch, it's wise to send a quick thank you note.

Be sure to be genuine and avoid sending generic notes by thanking the investor specifically for something you learned from the interaction.

Sending a thank-you note shows humility and gratitude and keeps you in their good books (even if they don't invest now, they may in a future funding round).

According to Tej Lalvani (Dragon investor, Dragons Den 2017-21) you just need to nail four things:

1. **The numbers**: calculate them accurately, make sure they're achievable, then commit them to memory
2. **Honesty**: if there are aspects of your business you doubt, investors will find out. Account for them before they come up or adjust your numbers
3. **Humanity**: investors want to work with nice people! Don't just try to 'impress'; try to be your most relatable and friendly self
4. **Passion**: loving what you do is a key part of achieving success. Passion creates resilience, grit, and tenacity

3.16 7 Key SCALE UP models

Everybody starts their own business with a dream to rise above the stars. Businesses follow different models which they think are right. Selecting a suitable model for your business is an important step that determines the scalability of a business.

This can help you scale up by taking examples and action plans of successful enterprises. Let's jump right into some prominent examples of business models.

1. Freemium Business Model
In this business model, they offer some of their services free of cost and charge an amount for their premium packs. As you have given a taste of your product most of the customers will come back for more.

We can find this business model in action when we are relaxing with a cup of coffee and some sweet music on Spotify. Just when you relax into the calm tunes, you will hear the monotonous nagging to upgrade to premium for uninterrupted music.

By calculating what you can give away and what you can show to attract more premium customers, you are creating a great strategy for attracting more clients. This model always ensures a greater customer lifetime (the time which ensures the cash flow from the company).

But the biggest problem faced by this model is attracting the wrong type of customers. When you give things for free, the people who like free stuff will gather around. The real question for you will be, how to convince these people to upgrade to premium.

The flaw of the freemium model is that you would be depleting your cash flow by supporting non-paying customers. Even though a large number of users is an added advantage, we might be able to change these customers to paying ones but till that time you have to split your resources to help them.

The time, money and resources used in the transition of non-paying to paying customers would be troublesome. You would be riding the thin line of spending and acquiring assets.

2. Razor and Blade Business Model

This cheeky strategy involves pushing a primary product into the market at a low cost or free but the complimentary items will always be at a high price. That's why the name razor and blade model, the primary product razor is at low cost when considering the price of the blades.

This model is also adopted by ink cartridge companies and so on. Apple took this business model but they 'thought differently' and changed it. They push their primary product at a much higher rate compared to its complimentary items. This model is the reverse razor and blade model.

This is an ideal business model if your customer revenue is based on the usage of your product but like every other business model this also has a drawback. The downside of this model is its competition when the basic product does not meet customer expectations they can always go with a different brand.

3. Crowdsourcing Business Model

Many believe population is a huge drawback of humanity, but this business model changes that perception.

As the name suggests, crowdsourcing gathers services from a group of people who may be hired professionals from other companies to customers through voting, microtasks, etc

You can outsource your work to places where labour is affordable and with the added advantage of innovative ideas from a whole new set of people.

Legos uses this business model by giving the opportunity to the customers to design their own toys.

By doing this they are literally getting new ideas from the customers, which is a great way to understand what the market wants because you are taking suggestions from the market, and who better understands the market other than the market itself.

But with the power of quantity there comes a cost in quality, as there are a lot of people doing tasks there would be plagiarised products, substandard items, etc. and there will also be problems related to confidentiality.

4. Franchising Business Model

Ever wondered when you walk into every Starbucks it's the same theme, same colour, and the same menu for all their outlets? This is the franchise business model in action.

People can make deals with companies like Starbucks, Apple, etc to sell the company products or services with the company trademark, knowledge, and process for a franchising fee. This gives your business the opportunity to scale up to a global level without your personal supervision or your talent pool.

Even when this is freeing, you should remember some downfalls of this model. There is a high chance for legal disputes because you enter into a business agreement with other people and any disputes must be resolved in mediation or court system.

The franchising agreement should be airtight because when you are the franchisor you need to look after your brand and property.

5. Peer-to-Peer Business Model

How many cars does Uber own? How many hotels does Airbnb own?

None. Yet they are the largest taxi and hotel services there are now.

These are examples of peer-to -peer business models where a company acts as the middleman between the consumer and the producer. Companies like Uber, by collecting a fee for their services provide customers a direct link to their service provider and saves them from the hassle of finding these on their own.

The peer-to-peer model actually thrives from the idea to make the customer's life easier and we humans like things handed to us. So as long as humans exist, the peer-to-peer model has the ability to scale up.

The main problem with this business model is that the customer is never in contact with the seller, so there is a chance of online fraud like counterfeit products, and a case of security of the customers personal information.

No seller can be added to the marketplace without proper background checks. Security is a main concern in this business model.

6. Subscription Business Model

This is the business model for people out there who want to receive regular payments from their customers and make a solid cash flow.

Here the companies provide access to their services for a period of time at a price and the customer needs to renew this at recurring intervals.

Netflix is a great example for a company that follows this business model. They collect money to access their exclusive contents.

This business model has a high scalability rate as the contents once created need not be reproduced to serve each consumer. You just give access and done, that's it. These customers will come to you to renew their subscription if it's worthwhile. This ensures a higher customer lifetime.

Subscription model is great in getting a regular income but here is something to think about before you use this model.

Maintaining a subscription model is hard. You have to regularly update your contents, or your subscribers will drop out. Furthermore, in the start-up phase you really need to convince the customers of the value of your product or service to bag subscribers.

7. Bundling Business Model

Bundling happens when companies with different products and services come together to provide you with a service as a single combined unit.

McDonald's Happy Meals have Lego toys, soda, etc in them, each is provided by different companies but served as a single product. This model increases the revenue by simplifying the decision of customers who have a difficult time to pick.

Providing more related services in a single place will attract customers and help in selling the product, of different brands, as a bundle. And this will also ensure greater customer satisfaction.

Scalability opportunities arise here when bundling with the right companies can introduce you to a new market of possibilities and the chance to grow exponentially.

No matter how great a model is, there will be some drawbacks. Here, as the products come in a bundle, people who want only one product would be reluctant to buy the bundle and so the selection of products is crucial.

8. Ecommerce Business Model

E-Commerce is a business model with a lot of branches, but the core of the model lies in the hands of the internet. You can show your product to a wider audience than the local market and gather their orders online.

By collecting the basic details they can send the product to the person or company. Jeff Bezos will have a few words to talk about this model as Amazon "is" E-Commerce.

The opportunity to scale up is immense because of the internet. Everybody can see everything through it. And with eCommerce, people can now shop for anything of their desire that may be halfway around the world.

The things to remember while using this business model is that you are using the internet for your business and all the problems associated with it will be your problem too. Like site crashes, security, lack of privacy, etc will be a problem for you.

9. Aggregator Business Model

In the Aggregator Business model, an aggregator collects information on goods and services from various competing sources and makes them their partner. Here the aggregator provides the best user experience for the customers and thus increasing the market for manufacturers.

If you doubt the scalability of this model, then I suggest you look at Amazon and Uber. Scaling up is inevitable in this model because, if successful, it will always attract a huge audience and you need not worry about the production side. The platform doesn't need to be manufactured again and again for every new user.

Takeaway

The world is full of opportunities to scaleup your business. And businesses that scale-up have a model that is similar to the idea of passive income (a source of income that makes money even while you are asleep), scaling without intensive supervision.

These are a few models you can consider while looking for ways to improve your business or start-up. Your business model is your action plan, so plan wisely and aim for global acceptance.

There is a multi-award-winning book simply named **Scaling up** *by Verne Harnish.*

This book is written so everyone can get aligned in contributing to the growth of a firm. There's no reason to do it alone, yet many top leaders feel like they are the ones dragging the rest of the organization up the S-curve of growth.

There is also a fabulous book on Business modelling by *Alexander Osterwalder* named **Business Model Generation.**

Business Model Generation is a practical, inspiring handbook for anyone striving to improve a business model or craft a new one.

It features a tightly integrated, visual, lie-flat design that enables immediate hands-on use and is designed for those ready to abandon outmoded thinking and embrace new, innovative models of value creation: executives, consultants, entrepreneurs, and leaders of all organizations.

Chapter Four:

Marketing Management

4.8 Cost Of Acquisition

Customer Acquisition Cost: The One Metric That Can
Determine Your Company's Fate

Customer Acquisition Cost (CAC) is a metric that has been
growing in use, along with the emergence of Internet
companies and web-based advertising campaigns that can be
tracked.

Traditionally, a company had to engage in shotgun style
advertising and find methods to track consumers through the
decision-making process.

Today, many web-based companies can engage in highly
targeted campaigns and track consumers as they progress
from interested leads to long-lasting loyal customers. In this
environment, the CAC metric is used by both companies and
investors.

What the CAC Metric means to You

As mentioned above, the CAC metric is important to two parties: companies and investors. The first party includes outside early-stage investors who use it to analyse the scalability of business. They can determine a company's profitability by looking at the difference between how much money can be extracted from customers and the costs of extracting it.

The other party interested in the metric is an internal operations or marketing specialist. They use it to optimize the return on their advertising investments. In other words, if the costs to extract money from customers can be reduced, the company's profit margin improves, and it makes a larger profit.

Then, investors are more interested in providing the company with the resources it needs, partners are more committed to growth, and the company can use the improved profit margins to pass the value to its customers or shareholders.

How you can measure CAC

Basically, the CAC can be calculated by simply dividing all the costs spent on acquiring more customers (marketing expenses) by the number of customers acquired in the period the money was spent. For example, if a company spent £1500 on marketing in a year and acquired 100 customers in the same year, their CAC is £15.00.

There are caveats about using this metric that you should be aware of when applying it. For instance, a company may have made investments on marketing that it does not expect to see results from until a later period. While these instances are rare, it may cloud the relationship when calculating the CAC.

It is suggested that you perform multiple variations to account for these situations. However, I will provide some examples of calculating the CAC metric in its most practical and simple form with two examples. The first company (Example 1) has a poor metric. The second (Example 2) has a great one.

EXAMPLE

Example 1: An ecommerce company

In this example, we take a fictitious ecommerce company that sells organic food products. The company spent £10,000 on advertising last month, and its marketing team says 1,000 new orders were placed. This suggests a CAC of £10, a figure that has no meaning.

If a Mercedes-Benz dealer has a CAC of £10, the management team will be delighted when looking at the year's financial statements.

However, in the case of this company, the average order placed by customers is £25.00, and it has a profit margin of 100% on all products. This means that on average, the company makes £12.50 per sale and generates £2.50 from each customer to pay for salaries, web hosting, office space, and other general expenses.

While this is the quick and dirty calculation, what happens if customers make more than one purchase over their lifetime? What if they completely stop shopping at bricks and mortar grocery stores and buy from only this company?

The purpose of customer lifetime value (CLV) is specifically designed to resolve this. You can find a CLV calculator by simply searching in your favourite search engine. In general, this metric helps you form a more accurate understanding of what the customer acquisition cost means to your company.

A £10.00 customer acquisition cost may be quite low if customers make a £25.00 purchase every week for 20 years! Or they might struggle to keep customers with most only making one purchase.

Example 2: An online software company

The company in this example provides downloadable software which provides virus protection for PC's. The cost of distributing the software is low since it is cloud-based, and customers need little support. Moreover, it can easily retain customers because of the pain customers would experience if they didn't have this in place.

The company has worked its way up the search engines and has an expert sales support team working for minimum wage, based out of their overseas technical support desk. The company also has many strategic partnerships that provide a steady supply of customers. In fact, they spend only £2.00 acquiring a new customer with a lifetime value of £2,000. Here is the calculation:

Total cost of technical support call centres: £1,000,000/year

Total cost paid to strategic alliance partners per customer: £1.00

Total monthly spending on search engine optimization: £20,000/year

Total new customers generated in the year: 1,020,000

Customer acquisition cost: (£1,020,000 / 1,020,000 customers) + £1.00 per customer = £2.00

As in our previous example, the amount is worth only the money extracted from customers. This company has used a customer retention calculation to determine that its customer lifetime value (CLV) is £2,000. That means this company can turn a £2.00 investment into £2,000 of revenue! This is both attractive to investors and a signal to the marketing team that an effective system is in place.

What About CAC Per Marketing Channel?
Knowing the CAC for each of your marketing channels is what most marketers want to know. If you know which channels have the lowest CAC, you know where to double on your marketing spend. The more you can allocate your marketing budget into lower CAC channels, the more customers you can obtain for a fixed budget amount.

The simple approach is to break out your spreadsheet and gather all your marketing receipts for the year, quarter, or month (however you want to do it) – and add up those amounts by channel. For example, how much did you spend on Google AdWords and Facebook advertising? In this case, you might put this in a column called "PPC" or "Pay-Per-Click". How much did you spend on SEO and blogging? This might go into a column called "Inbound Marketing Costs".

Now that you know how much you spent on each channel, you can apply a simplistic formula and assume each channel "worked" to get the same number of customers as the next channel. This would be an averaging method. The only issue is that it can be difficult to know what channel is responsible for which customers.

You can easily see where this approach becomes futile. Say you only ran one Pay-Per-Click advertisement on one day – just as a test. You spent £10 total and that's all. When you look at your spreadsheet, it will appear Pay-Per-Click would be the best marketing channel because of its extremely low CAC. It would be unwise to double on Pay-Per-Click because you know you really didn't utilize it all for that period.

For ecommerce companies that sell physical products, it's easy to know what Pay-Per-Click advertisements lead to direct sales because of the conversion tracking the advertising platform provides. In this case, you can determine that value and note this in your spreadsheet. This will give you a better idea of how your Pay-Per-Click campaigns are doing relative to the rest of your marketing spend.

Also, with tools like customer analytics, you can trace paying customers back to their "last touch" attribution source. This means you can see the last channel the customer visited before doing their first sales with your online business.

For example, if a customer came from an organic search result, you would know that SEO would be responsible for that customer acquisition.

This is where marketing gets philosophical :)

One school of thought is that each marketing channel supports the next channel – it's a combined effort. Your blog posts reinforce your Pay-Per-Click ads, and all channels work together to bring in customers. This is a common notion in outdoor advertising. Billboards reinforce T.V. campaigns, which reinforce radio spots and so on. Ultimately it comes down to your own company's philosophy on how to attribute customer acquisition.

If you feel that last touch is "good enough," you can use that model for your CAC calculations.

However, you may have wildly popular viral videos (think Dollar Shave Club) or a blog that drives a lot of word-of-mouth referrals. These obviously support your overall marketing efforts and tend to be more difficult to track and attribute to customer acquisition.

How You Can Improve CAC

We all wish that our company was like Example 2. The reality is that our advertising campaigns can always be more effective, customer loyalty can always be improved, and more value can always be extracted from consumers. There are several methods your business can use to improve its CAC in its industry:

Improve on-site conversion metrics:

One may set up goals on Google Analytics and perform A/B split testing with new checkout systems to reduce shopping cart abandonment rate and improve the landing page, site speed, mobile optimization, and other factors to enhance overall site performance.

Enhance user value:

By the highly conceptual notion of "user value," we mean the ability to generate something pleasing to the users. This may be additional feature enhancements/qualities that consumers have expressed interest in. It may be implementing something to improve the existing product for greater positioning or developing new ways to make money from existing customers. For instance, you may realize that customer satisfaction ratings have a positive correlation with retention rate.

Implement customer relationship management (CRM):

Nearly all successful companies that have repeat buyers implement some form of CRM. This may be a complex sales team using a cloud-based sales tracking system, automated email lists, blogs, loyalty programs, and/or other techniques that capture customer loyalty.

4.9 Lifetime value

How to Calculate Customer Lifetime Value

Customer lifetime value (LTV) is one of the most important metrics to measure at any growing company. By measuring LTV in relation to cost of customer acquisition (CAC), companies can measure how long it takes to recoup the investment required to earn a new customer -- such as the cost of sales and marketing.

If you want your business to acquire and retain highly valuable customers, then it's essential that your team learn what customer lifetime value is and how to calculate it.

Customer lifetime value is the metric that indicates the total revenue a business can reasonably expect from a single customer account. It considers a customer's revenue value and compares that number to the company's predicted customer lifespan. Businesses use this metric to identify significant customer segments that are the most valuable to the company.

LTV tells companies how much revenue they can expect one customer to generate over the course of the business relationship. The longer a customer continues to purchase from a company, the greater their lifetime value becomes.

This is something that customer support and success teams have direct influence over during the customer's journey. Customer support reps and customer success managers play key roles in solving problems and offering recommendations that influence customers to stay loyal to a company - or to churn.

How to Calculate LTV

To calculate customer lifetime value, you need to calculate average purchase value, and then multiply that number by the average purchase frequency rate to determine customer value. Then, once you calculate average customer lifespan, you can multiply that by customer value to determine customer lifetime value.

Getting stuck with the math? Let's break it down step-by-step.

Customer Lifetime Value Model

Calculate average purchase value:

Calculate this number by dividing your company's total revenue in a time (usually one year) by the number of purchases over the course of that same time.

Calculate average purchase frequency rate:

Calculate this number by dividing the number of purchases over the course of the time by the number of unique customers who made purchases during that period.

Calculate customer value:

Calculate this number by multiplying the average purchase value by the average purchase frequency rate.

Calculate average customer lifespan:

Calculate this number by averaging out the number of years a customer continues purchasing from your company.

Then, calculate LTV by multiplying customer value by the average customer lifespan. This will give you an estimate of how much revenue you can reasonably expect an average customer to generate for your company over the course of their relationship with you.

Improving Customer Lifetime Value

Now that you know your customer lifetime value, how do you improve it? While there are several ways to gain revenue, customer satisfaction and customer retention are two keyways to increase your customer's LTV.

Customer Satisfaction

Making your customers happier will usually result in them spending more money at your company. According to Research, 55% of growing companies think it's "very important" to invest in customer service programs. If we look at companies with stagnant or decreasing revenue, only 29% said this investment was "very important." Companies that are actively geared towards their customer's success are experiencing more revenue because of increased customer satisfaction.

Customer Retention

Acquiring a new customer can be a costly affair. In fact, an article published by Harvard Business Review, found that gaining a customer can cost anywhere between five and 25 times more than retaining an existing one. Additionally, a further study found that a 5% increase in retention rate can lead to an increase in profit between 25% to 95%.

This makes it imperative that your business identifies and nurtures the most valuable customers that interact with your company. By doing so, you'll gain more total revenue resulting in an increase in customer lifetime value.

4.10 Irresistible converting offers?

The offer is the most important things in a marketing campaign.

If you're not communicating what you're offering, if it's not clear and if it's something that no one wants, then no one is going to buy it or respond to your marketing or advertising. It's that simple; it's the most critical part of your campaign.

Therefore, the big question is; where do you start in creating that irresistible offer?

First you must know what your objective is. Effective selling solves problems, so your objective should be to turn the solution into a killer offer. Think about some of the best offers you've seen, when an ad compelled you to buy something that you didn't think you'd buy. Those are the best examples of irresistible offers. Creating an irresistible offer that converts prospects to buyers is integral to any marketing campaign.

What Makes a Really Good Offer?

The short answer is simple: A good offer must be an easy decision. What you're offering is of such tremendous value that it creates desire, which turns into action of some sort (download, purchase, register for an event or webinar, schedule a consultation).

The goal is to give someone an offer they can't refuse. Keep in mind, this is only going to make sense if someone is in the market for a solution. You can only solve a problem if someone has that problem. But then again, someone is probably not going to be searching for a product or solution if they don't need it.

What Does a Compelling Offer Look Like?

In general, some of the most effective offers are ones that give prospects a chance to test a product – a 14-day free trial, 30-day free trial, free demo, even a scaled-down version of the full product. To find an offer, look at what the competitors in your niche are doing. One tactic to use to learn this is to Google the company name and see what their Ad Words offer is.

Awareness Is the Difference

Someone who is googling Salesforce may not have any idea about Pipedrive until they see the name come up in the search results. Then when they go to search Pipedrive, they already have an awareness about the brand. Awareness is the difference.

When someone already knows the name of a brand, are still in the looking around phase and are not sure whether a product is for them, they are considered Product-Aware. However, when they are looking for a competitor, they are considered Solution-Aware. Your challenge is to move prospects from Product Awareness to Solution Awareness in YOUR favour as efficiently as possible, which is why the pressure lies on your offer.

Our Top 15 Favourite Irresistible Offers

1. Templates & checklist
2. Video or audio download
3. Cheat sheet or handout
4. Quick start kit
5. Free trial
6. Vault, library access
7. Physical giveaway
8. Gated content
9. Webinar
10. Event tickets
11. Email course
12. First/sample chapter
13. Free coaching session
14. PDF version of something
15. Free shipping

Which of the ones listed above will work for you?

Trick question – ALL of them, can and do work right now. You need to invest the time to understand your prospect and their biggest pain points, then develop an irresistible offer that best addresses them.

Some of our favourites are:

Webinar – Low risk, free education, or training, can be evergreen (automated); the difference between webinar and watching a video – a webinar is more of an event so people will have more respect for the event, resulting in higher attendance and participation.

Template & Checklist – This is an uncomplicated way to collect email addresses. The prospect can download it, it is easy and inexpensive to create; depending on client LTV, can send as direct mail (laminated).

Physical giveaway – This is the Dan Kennedy "bulky mail" approach. Do something that makes you stand out and you'll gain attention. Ship a relevant book for free, the prospect pays shipping (the "free + shipping" offer). LTV increases because people end up buying the software.

Cheat sheet – These are easy to create, and a prospect can look at in a couple of minutes. It is an MVP = Minimal Viable Product; create it, put on a landing page, and see if people will bite.

Live events – People have multiple browsers open on multiple devices at the same time, but if you offer a live event, people are forced to give you, their attention.

Creating an irresistible offer is the crux of any successful marketing campaign and is integral to the success of a product and company. Done correctly, an irresistible offer will bring people to you because they are confident (or are ready to be convinced) that you have the solution to address their problems.

How confident are you in the effectiveness of your irresistible offer? Are your conversion rates as high as you'd like them to be? Is your advertising spend going to waste?

4.11 Positioning

Becoming an authority within your sector/industry can often be a lifetimes work. However, we all must start somewhere, and it began the moment someone approached and asked "Can you tell me..."

4 simple ways to begin to become an authority in your niche

Becoming an authority in your field is a terrific way to stand out from the competition and position yourself as a go-to thought leader. It unlocks career opportunities you would never imagine and levels of success you wouldn't necessarily reach otherwise. And it all starts with giving.

Sharing your experience, thoughts, suggestions is a fantastic way of showing others your abilities and willingness to support others.

It then becomes a matter of staying consistent with building your personal brand and finding opportunities to share your knowledge.

1. Be active on LinkedIn and update your profile

With its excellent features (i.e., content and education tools and growing user base), LinkedIn has become the network for professional growth. Many tend to use it to update their profile with new jobs and connect with people they won't necessarily develop a relationship with.

Doing only this will have you miss the incredible opportunity LinkedIn provides to tell your story, highlight your knowledge, and become an influential personality in your industry. To start taking advantage of these opportunities, start becoming more active on the platform. This means writing and sharing articles, engaging in relevant conversations on your newsfeed, and getting to know the people in your network.

Gone are the days when your LinkedIn profile was just a copy-and-paste version of your resume

Now is the time to start being seen in every activity that is trending in your industry. And it all boils down to showing some personality and using all its tools consistently.

2. Share your thoughts on other outlets

Leverage the power of existing audiences to gain visibility. When you become a guest contributor, you not only expand your reach, but you also become more credible. Earning a spot-on reputable outlet is, of course, no easy feat. But if you have an interesting perspective and provide valuable content for their audience, you will increase your chances. Editors are always on the lookout for contributed pieces and have an appreciation for unique angle, so that's where you come in.

3. Pitch yourself as guest on podcasts

Podcasting continues to be upwardly growing in both number of podcasters and number of those subscribing. There is definitely an audience here. And similar to contributing to outlets, being featured on podcasts can help you build your personal brand. Whether your field is in public policy, healthcare, digital marketing, there is a podcast for every niche, and you will find the right place to share your expertise. These modern-day radio shows provide a golden opportunity to reach a massive audience interested in what you have to say.

4. Teach online classes and workshops

One of the most effective, yet often overlooked, ways of establishing authority in your niche is having online classes and workshops. If the thought intimidates you, but you aspire to that, start small with hosting a virtual summit. Otherwise known as an online conference featuring expert speakers, a virtual summit is a proven method for growing a community and demonstrating your expertise. It's great way of making yourself known for all industry-related news and insights.

4.12 Raining referrals

A referral program is a deliberate, systematic way of getting people to make referrals to your business. Referral programs reward existing customers for sharing word-of-mouth and incentivise new customers to try out your brand, increasing long term revenue whether for products or services.

Your customers may refer more if the incentive gets better each time, they use their referral link. Therefore, tier rewards work well. ... For example, you can create a program so the reward is dependent on how many approved referrals your customer sends. Your customer could earn £25 for their first 5 Referrals, but £50 for the next 10 and £75 for the next 20.

One of the basic beliefs of customer success is using your service to create advocates for your business. A happy army of satisfied customers can do a lot of legwork for you. And when word-of-mouth referrals make up 20-50% of most purchasing decisions (especially for new businesses and in emerging markets) why not take advantage of the opportunity?

But there's a catch: assuming your customers will refer you to their connections simply because you provide exceptional service is idealistic at best. Referrals only happen out of the good of a customer's heart some of the time - for the rest of it, giving customers a reason to refer will work wonders. As with most things in business, a plan is necessary.

If you're looking to grow your business, retain the customers you already have, and reach your revenue goals, it's time to implement a customer referral program. Simply having one is good business sense because it reveals two things:

1. That you're confident enough in your services and team to know that a referral program would be a positive investment and
2. You know that despite your good service, some customers might need a push to go out of their way for you.

How valuable is a referral?

A customer referral is highly valuable because it doesn't cost you much (if anything) to acquire them. The exact value of a referral varies across different businesses, but it's roughly the lifetime value (LTV) of a typical customer, plus the typical cost of customer acquisition (CAC), which you can then use to acquire additional new customers.

The reality is, however, that you're effectively asking your customers to stand in place of your marketing and sales departments. And when referrals are the heart of generating new business, operating with tact, consistency, and patience is extremely important.

7 Steps to start an effective Customer Referral Program

1. Set Your Goals

Ask yourself:

- what do you hope to get out of this referral program?
- Are your goals tied more to growth and revenue?
- Do you want to add retention to that mix?
- Are you in an industry that requires an exceptional amount of trust-building?

Once you decide what your goals are -- and explicitly define them - the next steps should lay themselves out for you:

Discover how (if at all) referrals have been coming to your business.

Involve marketing, sales management, support - anyone who would be responsible for building customer relationships -- and assess how they've been traditionally dealing with referrals. This will give you an idea of where you already are.

Do a little maths

What's an existing customer worth?

Compared to time spent monitoring and managing onboarding programs, how many referrals do you need to break even? A 10% conversion rate for referrals is, on average, a good starting point (and this, of course, is dependent on your business size and growth goals).

2. List Possible Referral Sources

We'll call these advocates, and they can be anyone who you're already connected with in the present, or who you have been connected to in the past. Begin listing them. This list could include current customers, past customers, leads that may not have closed, industry leaders, your vendors, etc. This will give you solid footing to start out with.

3. Plan to Reach Out

Now, refine. Narrow down the list of advocates and sources to a list of "inner circle" contacts. These are people who know what value your business has and would refer you without any incentive. Finding your inner circle isn't a process that can be automated - you'll get more benefit from this if you pull and segment these contacts manually.

Once you have your inner circle segmented out, you now have two things to take into consideration:

- **Timing is everything**

Identify appropriate times to ask these inner circle advocates to take part in your referral program. Because they are people you've worked with before, this is a less strenuous process starting out. When you start working with people who will need an incentive (which we talk about below), it's important to consider the relationship. For some companies, depending on the service or product, asking for a referral needs to happen late in the relationship. For others, it could be upon the first sale (think apps, digital interface services).

Then, once you've asked, wait some more. That might require a waiting period of months, or even a year, to remind them about the referral program again.

- **Not all referrals are equal**

Be meticulous with your advocates (even your inner circle ones). Identify people who you think could market your brand the way that it should be marketed. Within that inner circle, who do you have a stellar, standout relationship with? Or do you have an existing customer that came from a referral and worked out? And remember: Watch out for referral fatigue, and make sure you're not overburdening your contacts.

4. Identify Your Incentives

There are two options for a referral program:

- an incentive
- and a non-incentive program.

A University study found that non-cash incentives are 24% more effective at boosting performance than cash incentives. During this step, you should break your contacts out by levels and decide which ones can receive which offer.

And don't forget the referrer -- make sure they get something out of the deal, too. Take Airbnb for example: when a customer refers a friend, they get £20 credit -- and when a customer first signs up, they get a credit towards their first trip over a certain amount.

5. Create Resources to Alert Your Customers

Once you have a referral program, create resources you think would work well, and alert your customers. Then, promote, promote, promote. And consider multiple avenues of promotion beyond the time-limited email campaign to remind your customers of the program's existence.

Those might look like:

- Newsletters
- Blogs
- CTAs & Email Signatures
- Product updates
- Once you have the referral programs outlined, you'll have an idea of what resources you need for each one. I've listed out a few resources you might need below:
- Emails for each type of contact telling them about your referral program
- A message explaining what types of customers fit well with your business. You need to paint a picture in their minds of your ideal customer
- A workflow that leads your contacts through the program and alerts your sales team when to call
- A landing page that provides a place for your contacts to give you their friend's information
- Scripts for your sales and customer support teams to follow when explaining your referral programs
- A referral kit filled with resources for your contacts to share with their friends: this can include case studies, testimonials, eBooks, videos, anything that gives insight into working with your business

Whatever your medium, make sure it's consistent, persistent (though not over-the-top) and in line with your program's revenue, growth, and retention goals.

6. Set Up Tracking

Regardless of the size of your company (though this is especially relevant if your company has a larger customer base) you need to have tracking set in place. This will ensure that you don't miss one detail -- for referred accounts especially. You should be tracking:

- Who was referred and who referred them
- When they were referred
- Whether or not they converted or were sold
- How you're going to nurture and follow up with them, etc.

If you don't already invest in a CRM (customer relationship management) system, then now is a great time to become familiar! Keeping track of customer relationships is a huge component of customer success - the ability to individualize each account or relationship makes each customer feel like they're a unique part of your base.

7. Say Thank You

Thank the referrer for helping you out (this is where incentives might work, but also consider messaging, that thanks them specifically as well) and thank the referred for joining.

Then, get to work - you've got happy customers to prove right.

EXAMPLE

"Who do YOU know that ought to own a copy of THIS book? Email iwantto@addazero.co.uk with the subject "Referral" so that we can send them a copy with your compliments!

4.13 Guarantee's

A guarantee can be powerful. And just like a chainsaw, when used right, can cut through customer objections. However, used badly, it simply cuts through profit margins!

When and why do guarantees work?

Guarantees don't always increase sales. To understand when a guarantee would help, consider the two major functions of a guarantee:

- Function 1: A guarantee reduces the risk for the customer. If the company doesn't fulfil the guarantee's promise, the customer is compensated.
- Function 2: A good guarantee self-evidently promises that your business will be harmed if you don't honour your claims. It effectively says, "Our promise must be true. Otherwise, we wouldn't be in business." It thus acts as a kind of proof.

Many people underestimate the importance of Function 2.

Guarantees are most effective when...

- the visitors want what the company is promising,
- but they are nervous about the risk, or are sceptical about the claims,
- and your service does live up to its claims.

A 9-step checklist for implementing a guarantee safely

Is your company hesitant to offer a bold guarantee? That's understandable. A guarantee can do harm if it's implemented badly. Also, the feedback loop is long, because you can't calculate the costs of invoked guarantees until after the guarantee period has expired.

The following workflow provides a low-risk way to implement a bold guarantee:

Create the guarantee, based on the principles described above.

Carry out scenario modelling, as follows:

1. Create a table in which the columns represent different values of "Uplift in conversion," and the rows represent different values of "Percentage of customers who invoke the guarantee."
2. Then work out the net change in profit for each combination. Also consider how guarantee claims would be handled operationally (accepting returns, restocking shelves, issuing refunds, etc.). If you are satisfied that the guarantee will generate additional profits, then proceed to the next step.
3. Run the guarantee as an A/B-test for a brief time—for just a few days if that's all the risk you can bear.
4. Wait for the guarantee period to expire.
5. Calculate the increase in profits, based on the measured uplift in sales.
6. Calculate the cost of people invoking the guarantee. In our experience, the invocation rate tends to be lower than companies expect, sometimes by an order of magnitude.
7. If you need more data (which you probably will), return to Step 3 and run the guarantee for longer. By doing this in small increments, you remove the risk caused by the long feedback loop.
8. If you do have enough data, and the increase in profit more than offsets the cost of returns, make the guarantee permanent.
9. Return to Step 1, creating a bolder guarantee.

4.14 Follow up, Follow up, Follow up

You have automated Sales and Follow-up funnels embedded within your business?

What is a sales funnel?

A sales funnel is the marketing term for the journey potential customers go through on the way to purchase. There are several steps to a sales funnel, usually known as the top, middle, and bottom of the funnel, although these steps may vary depending on a company's sales model.

Any business owner knows the pain of just missing a sale. After weeks of pitches and demos, chatter and charm, the prospect drops out of the sales funnel without buying.

It happens. But it happens less often when you have the right sales funnel management help. Many small business sales funnels are more like sieves, with holes left by patched-together spreadsheets, sticky notes, missed appointments and forgotten follow-ups.

There's a better way. Sales and marketing automation software can plug those sales funnel holes and turn near-misses into sales.

A sales funnel is the marketing term for the journey your potential customers go through on their way to a purchase. You start with a lot of potential customers who may have heard of your product or service. A smaller part of that group may want to learn more, and a smaller part of that group may contact you.

As the process goes on, you're talking to fewer people who are more interested, until you end up with the people who become customers.

The first of the sales funnel stages is called the "awareness" level, because it's where people first become aware of your product or service. They may hear about you from your advertising, social media, even word of mouth.

How and why those people move down the funnel depends on your own sales and marketing ability, of course. The leads in the middle and lower sales funnel stages are those that you want to pay the most attention to, because they've moved beyond awareness to interest.

Find the cracks in your sales funnel stages

Now we start to see why sales funnel management matters. Even very good prospects can leak out of the sales funnel along the way if they're not nurtured carefully. The best way to prevent that loss is to have a clear idea of the steps in your sales process—and help in making those steps happen.

Now we start to see why sales funnel management matters. Even particularly good prospects can leak out of the sales funnel along the way if they're not nurtured carefully. The best way to prevent that loss is to have a clear idea of the steps in your sales process—and help in making those steps happen.

Sales funnel leaks often spring from three basic causes. The good news is that sales funnel management can help with each.

Throwing away the "no's" too quickly

In sales, a "no" can often mean "not until later." For example, a common objection for customer relationship management (CRM) software is this: "I don't have time to get my content together to make the platform useful." This prospect is saying, "I'm interested, I see the value, but I can't take advantage of it at this moment."

It's tempting to dump this lead and move on to the next.

There's a better solution: Build out an automated email follow-up campaign that speaks directly to this objection. Any time you encounter this problem, you can send that prospect information that seems designed just for them. A multi-month educational campaign may reduce their content anxiety and nurture them toward a sale. Yes, it's work up front, but once finished, this campaign will work for you always.

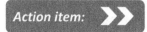

Look at the most common objections from your prospects and think about which can be turned around with helpful education and automated follow-up. Where in your sales funnel are you dismissing prospects too quickly?

Follow-up fails

Are you following up as much as you should be? Probably not, says the Business News Daily:

48% of sales reps never follow up with prospects

Only 10% of sales reps make more than three contacts with a prospect

Yet 80% of sales close between the fifth and 12th contact

That's a lot of follow-up fails. The challenge is easy to understand: Do I call new leads, or follow up with an old one for the sixth time? Persistence can feel like a waste of time, but the numbers prove otherwise.

But there's a better solution: small businesses may find help lies in a marketing automation funnel. Instead of an either/or game, automation software offers a both/and game. All your prospects get consistent and friendly emails and contacts at all stages, so you can save your personal attention for the day's hottest leads.

Action item: »

Analyse your last 20 leads and count how many times, on average, you contacted a prospect. If you see follow-up fails, a marketing automation funnel can help.

Too slow

Did you know that new leads are nine times more likely to convert if you follow up within the first five minutes after they express interest? Wait 30+ minutes, and your lead is 21 times less likely to turn into a sale.

You may be asking, "How the heck am I supposed to contact a lead within the first five minutes? That seems impossible."

There's a better solution: It's possible with sales funnel management automation. Set up your system with the response you want, and it will be ready to send it immediately to any interested prospect—even the one who contacts you on Saturday at 3 am. As captured leads pass down the funnel, your sales automation platform can send added personalized emails that are right for each moment.

Action item: »

Figure out how quickly you normally respond to a brand-new prospect right now. Then craft your first mass personalized email to send to prospects.

4.15 Marketing Pillars

The 7 Ps of Marketing

Once you've developed your marketing strategy, there is a "Seven P Formula" you should use to continually evaluate and revaluate your business activities.

These seven are:

1. **PRODUCT**
2. **PRICE**
3. **PROMOTION**
4. **PLACE**
5. **PACKAGING**
6. **POSITIONING**
7. **PEOPLE**

As products, markets, customers and needs change rapidly, you must continually revisit these seven Ps to make sure you're on track and achieving the maximum results possible for you in today's marketplace.

Product

To begin with, develop the habit of looking at your product as though you were an outside marketing consultant brought in to help your company decide whether it's in the right business at this time. Ask critical questions such as, "*Is your current product or service, or mix of products and services, appropriate and suitable for the market and the customers of today?*"

Whenever you're having difficulty selling as much of your products or services as you'd like, you need to develop the habit of assessing your business honestly and asking, "Are these the right products or services for our customers today?"

Is there any product or service you're offering today that, knowing what you now know, you would not bring out again today? Compared to your competitors, is your product or service superior in some significant way to anything else available? If so, what is it? If not, could you develop an area of superiority? Should you be offering this product or service at all in the current marketplace?

Prices

The second P in the formula is price. Develop the habit of continually examining and re-examining the prices of the products and services you sell to make sure they're still appropriate to the realities of the current market. Sometimes you need to lower your prices. At other times, it may be appropriate to raise your prices. Many companies have found that the profitability of certain products or services doesn't justify the amount of effort and resources that go into producing them. By raising their prices, they may lose a percentage of their customers, but the remaining percentage generates a profit on every sale. Could this be appropriate for you?

Sometimes you need to change your terms and conditions of sale. Sometimes, by spreading your price over a series of months or years, you can sell far more than you are today, and the interest you can charge will more than make up for the delay in cash receipts. Sometimes you can combine products and services together with exclusive offers and special promotions. Sometimes you can include free additional items that cost you little to produce but make your prices appear far more attractive to your customers.

In business, as in nature, whenever you experience resistance or frustration in any part of your sales or marketing plan, be open to revisiting that area. Be open to the possibility that your current pricing structure is not ideal for the current market. Be open to the need to revise your prices, if necessary, to remain competitive, to survive and thrive in a fast-changing marketplace.

Promotion

The third habit in marketing and sales is to think in terms of promotion all the time. Promotion includes all the ways you tell your customers about your products or services and how you then market and sell to them.

Slight changes in the way you promote and sell your products can lead to dramatic changes in your results. Even minor changes in your advertising can lead immediately to higher sales. Experienced copywriters can often increase the response rate from advertising by 500 percent by simply changing the headline on an advertisement.

Large and small companies in every industry continually experiment with diverse ways of advertising, promoting, and selling their products and services. And here is the rule: Whatever method of marketing and sales you're using today will, sooner or later, stop working. Sometimes it will stop working for reasons you know, and sometimes it will be for reasons you don't know. In either case, your methods of marketing and sales will eventually stop working, and you'll have to develop new sales, marketing and advertising approaches, offerings, and strategies.

Place

The fourth P in the marketing mix is the place where your product or service is sold. Develop the habit of reviewing and reflecting upon the exact location where the customer meets the salesperson. Sometimes a change in place can lead to a rapid increase in sales.

You can sell your product in many different places. Some companies use direct selling, sending their salespeople out to personally meet and talk with the prospect. Some sell by telemarketing. Some sell through catalogues or mail order. Some sell at trade shows or in retail establishments. Some sell in joint ventures with other related products or services. Some companies use manufacturers' representatives or distributors. Many companies use a combination of one or more of these methods.

In each case, the entrepreneur must make the right choice about the best location or place for the customer to receive essential buying information on the product or service needed to make a buying decision. What is yours? In what way should you change it? Where else could you offer your products or services?

Packaging

The fifth element in the marketing mix is the packaging. Develop the habit of standing back and looking at every visual element in the packaging of your product or service through the eyes of a critical prospect. Remember, people form their first impression about you within the first 30 seconds of seeing you or some element of your company. Small improvements in the packaging or external appearance of your product or service can often lead to completely different reactions from your customers.

Regarding the packaging of your company, your product or service, you should think in terms of everything that the customer sees from the first moment of contact with your company all the way through the purchasing process.

Packaging refers to the way your product or service appears from the outside. Packaging also refers to your people and how they dress and groom. It refers to your offices, your waiting rooms, your brochures, your correspondence, and every single visual element about your company. Everything counts. Everything helps or hurts. Everything affects your customer's confidence about dealing with you.

When IBM started under the guidance of Thomas J. Watson, Sr., he early concluded that fully 99 percent of the visual contact a customer would have with his company, at least initially, would be represented by IBM salespeople. Because IBM was selling relatively sophisticated high-tech equipment, Watson knew customers would have to have a high level of confidence in the credibility of the salesperson. He therefore instituted a dress and grooming code that became an inflexible set of rules and regulations within IBM.

As a result, every salesperson was required to look like a professional in every respect. Every element of their clothing-including dark suits, dark ties, white shirts, conservative hairstyles, shined shoes, clean fingernails-and every other feature gave off the message of professionalism and competence. One of the highest compliments a person could receive was, "You look like someone from IBM."

Positioning

The next P is positioning. You should develop the habit of thinking continually about how you are positioned in the hearts and minds of your customers. How do people think and talk about you when you're not present? How do people think and talk about your company? What positioning do you have in your market, in terms of the specific words people use when they describe you and your offerings to others?

In the famous book by Al Reis and Jack Trout, Positioning, the authors point out that how you are seen and thought about by your customers is the critical determinant of your success in a competitive marketplace. Attribution theory says that most customers think of you in terms of a single attribute, either positive or negative. Sometimes it's "service." Sometimes it's "excellence." Sometimes it's "quality engineering," as with Mercedes Benz. Sometimes it's "the ultimate driving machine," as with BMW. In every case, how deeply entrenched that attribute is in the minds of your customers and prospective customers determines how readily they'll buy your product or service and how much they'll pay.

Develop the habit of thinking about how you could improve your positioning. Begin by determining the position you'd like to have. If you could create the ideal impression in the hearts and minds of your customers, what would it be? What would you have to do in every customer interaction to get your customers to think and talk about in that specific way? What changes do you

need to make in the way interact with customers today to be seen as the best choice for your customers of tomorrow?

People

The final P of the marketing mix is people. Develop the habit of thinking in terms of the people inside and outside of your business who are responsible for every element of your sales, marketing strategies, and activities.

It's amazing how many entrepreneurs and businesspeople will work extremely hard to think through every element of the marketing strategy and the marketing mix, and then pay little attention to the fact that every single decision and policy must be carried out by a specific person, in a specific way. Your ability to select, recruit, hire and retain the proper people, with the skills and abilities to do the job you need to have done, is more important than everything else put together.

4.16 PPC

What Is PPC & How Does It Work?

If you have ever noticed the advertisements that appear alongside search results on Google and other search engines, you are already familiar with pay-per-click, or PPC advertising.

What Is Pay-Per-Click Advertising?

PPC is an online advertising model in which advertisers pay each time a user clicks on one of their online ads.

There are several types of PPC ads, but one of the most common types is the paid search ad. These ads appear when people search for things online using a search engine like Google – especially when they are performing commercial searches, meaning that they're looking for something to buy. This could be anything from a mobile search (someone looking for "pizza near me" on their phone) to a local service search (someone looking for a dentist or a plumber in their area) to someone shopping for a gift ("Mother's Day flowers") or a high-end item like enterprise software. All these search's trigger pay-per-click ads.

In pay-per-click advertising, businesses running ads are only charged when a user clicks on their ad, hence the name "pay-per-click."

Other forms of PPC advertising include display advertising (typically, serving banner ads) and remarketing.

How Does Pay-Per-Click Advertising Work?

For ads to appear alongside the results on a search engine (commonly referred to as a Search Engine Results Page, or SERP), advertisers cannot simply pay more to ensure that their ads appear more prominently than their competitor's ads. Instead, ads are subject to what is known as the Ad Auction, an entirely automated process that Google and other major search engines use to determine the relevance and validity of advertisements that appear on their SERPs.

How Keywords Work in Pay-Per-Click Advertising

As its name implies, the Ad Auction is a bidding system. This means that advertisers must bid on the terms they want to "trigger," or display, their ads. These terms are known as keywords.

Say, for example, that your business specializes in camping equipment. A user wanting to purchase a new tent, sleeping bag, or portable stove might enter the keyword "camping equipment" into a search engine to find retailers offering these items.

Now the user submits their search query, the search engine performs the complex algorithmic calculations that the Ad Auction is based upon. This determines which ads are displayed, in which order, and by which advertiser.

Since you must pay for each click on your ads, it's imperative to only bid on keywords that are relevant to your business, so you can be sure to get ROI from your ad spend. A keyword tool can help you find the right keywords to bid on that are both likely to drive sales or conversions and are not prohibitively expensive.

4.17 Landing pages

As you dive into the world of digital marketing, you'll likely encounter a whole new vocabulary and set of concepts. If you haven't already, you're bound to have questions about how landing pages fit into your digital marketing strategy. Developing a landing page sounds like a simple task, and it can be, but we want to stress that landing pages are vitally important to lead conversion.

What is a Landing Page?

A landing page is any web page that a consumer can land on, but in the marketing realm, it's usually a standalone page, distinct from your homepage or any other page, which serves a single and focused purpose. A landing page is a follow up to any promises that you've made in your content. Essentially, it's the next step toward a visitor becoming a customer. Your landing page lets you make a trade, some sort of exclusive offer, piece of information or a deal, in return for providing contact information.

Landing pages can be click through, leading to another page such as your e-commerce site, or lead generation based. Lead generation landing pages typically offer items like an eBook, free trial, contest entry or webinar registration in return for the submission of contact information. A good landing page will do its job by convincing a potential customer that it's worth it to provide personal details in return in exchange for whatever you have to offer. Landing pages can be found through a general search or via your company website, increasing the likelihood that a potential customer will end up there.

There's no need to have just one landing page, or even just one landing page at a time. In fact, experts in the marketing would probably suggest that you maintain multiple landing pages, targeted toward segmented customer populations.

Why Use Landing Pages?

You've done a great job building your brand and creating a website that represents it. Now you must make sure that all that hard work translates into sales. If you are looking for an effective lead conversion tool, landing pages are the way to go.

A landing page is a wonderful way to drive traffic, improve your SEO and build your brand.

A landing page is a great way to drive traffic, improve your SEO and build your brand. Approximately 68% of B2B businesses use landing pages to generate leads for future conversion. Fortunately for you, 44% of these clicks are directed toward home pages, which, as we'll discuss, is not a good strategy. Landing pages lead customers to a specific product, service or offer and encourage them to act. This is your opportunity to create conversions and build your customer base.

If landing pages are so important, why isn't every business using them? Well, there is a misconception that they are hard to create and maintain. Fortunately, that simply isn't true. Building an effective landing page is less about flashiness and more about getting the consumer what they're after.

What Makes a Good Landing Page?

First off, your home page should not be your landing page. You need to send prospective customers to a page that will let them take advantage of whatever exclusive offer you've promised them. Since they are tied to something specific, your landing pages have a better chance of capturing attention for a longer period. Good landing pages do several things:

1. They zero-in on the offer, not the company. Your future customers are clicking for a reason and duping them by not giving them what you've promised is not going to form a good first impression. Now is not the time to give a detailed history of your company. This isn't to say that the landing page should not be tied to your company brand. Just the opposite. They should serve a separate function, yet it should still be an extension of your brand.

2. They are focused and free of distractions. The content on your landing page should have the end-goal of getting the user what they want while completing the registration process

3. The forms are not intimidating. Lengthy forms can be daunting to visitors and may encourage them to move on, rather than take advantage of whatever opportunity you are offering. If you simply can't shorten your form, break it into steps, and let the user see exactly where they are in the process. For example, listing their name and address may be step one of four.

4. They speak to a specific audience. Segmenting your customer base helps you to target specific consumers through customized campaigns. If you have a base that's drawn to a particular offer, such as an eBook or discount, your landing page can serve as a built-in segmentation device, allowing you to nurture these leads effectively going forward.

5. They collect specific information about your prospective customers. Speaking of specific audiences, even if you draw the right crowd, they can't be converted if you don't collect the right information. The collection of demographic data should include more than simply a name and email address. It should also give you some idea of why a person clicked and what their long-term connection to your company might be.

6. They provide your exclusive offers with a home. Unless they are tied to landing pages, your online exclusive offers will do nothing to benefit your business. Creating landing pages provides a place for your offers to reside.

7. They provide a thank you. Your landing page should always be followed up with a thank you. This is not only polite but assures the consumer that they have completed the registration process.

8. They allow users access to other marketing channels. A customer likes what you've just offered. Now you can provide links to other offers, your social media profiles or an email list sign up.

There is no doubt about it, we are certainly living in a digitally connected world. Moving boldly forward with a digital marketing campaign can easily be one of the best investments that you make for your business. As you build your digital marketing toolbox, including landing pages is a smart move, and both you and your customers will reap the benefits.

Endless referrals *by Bob Burg*

Bob Burg has taught tens of thousands of sales professionals and entrepreneurs how to dramatically increase their business using powerful relationship-building techniques to build a referral business and gain clients. Burg introduces his Attraction Marketing System, a potent tool that brings the market for a product or service to the business through targeted initiatives using direct mail, email, telemarketing, websites, and other channels.

Invisible selling machine *by Ryan Deiss*

In the Invisible Selling Machine, entrepreneur, Ryan Deiss, walks you through all 5 phases of the prospect/customer lifestyle, and shows how each step can be automated and perpetuated to invisibly convert strangers into friends, friends into customers and customers into raving fans.

In short, if you want to grow your business and your customers just happen to have an email address... ...this book is for you.

Content Inc. *by Joe Pulizzi*

Survive and thrive in the marketplace without pitching your product. Learn how to build an online content platform that attracts new customers!

You'll discover how to:

Develop a model that creates an audience of future buyers Formulate a plan for social media sharing and search engine optimization Learn the six steps that power today's fastest growing businesses Catapult your company from micro status to becoming the leading industry player.

Chapter Five:
Money & Margins

5.7 Monthly Management Meetings

Where the following is an agenda item at EVERY meeting:

- **Sales**
- **Profits**
- **Budgets**
- **Cash-flow**

In my time as a coach, I have come across many companies who struggle to fully engage their managers and align them behind a common vision. This is a characteristic of many businesses. A Forbes article I recently read quotes a Gallup poll that reported that only 30% of workers are fully engaged; this is not surprising when you learn that only 36% of managers are engaged.

It for this reason the Monthly Management Meeting is so critical. This half-day meeting is your key to building the team, learning together, solving problems, working on specific issues, and reinforcing your company's culture, initiatives, and goals.

Here are some ideas on how to structure your Monthly Management Meetings:

1. Schedule them for the entire year in advance.

You might have them at the same day and time to make it easier on your team to get in the rhythm. For example, every first Thursday from 9-1 is always your Monthly Meeting. Attendance is not optional.

2. Allocate time to share good news in the beginning. It is a best practice to begin with some kind of 'check in/check out' around the room to get everyone engaged and talking in the meeting. This is usually more fun if you're focusing on something positive.
3. Provide a company update. This may be the entire agenda of the meeting if your Monthly Meeting is primarily to determine the new plan for the quarter.

If it is the middle of the quarter, your update time might be to share financial performance or an update on how your key initiatives are progressing over the quarter.

You might also include a brief time for updates from different departments, like marketing, operations, or sales, so that managers in various departments know what's happening in the company as a whole and aren't working in silos.

4. After the company update, the agenda typically varies. You might choose to either have a specific learning or training session for the team, or you might decide to work on solving a particular problem together. If you aren't sure what to work on, here are some ideas:

- Is there a part of your plan where your team are stuck? Not enough sales leads in the pipeline or not hitting your forecasted launch date on a big project. Maybe you spend an hour having all the managers just brainstorm 20 ways to solve the problem. You don't necessarily have to solve the problem in the meeting, but this gets your team thinking creatively and working together and gives you a chance to tap into their collective intelligence.

- Are you getting feedback from customers or employees that need to be addressed? Maybe you've had a lot of complaints or ideas for improvement about a particular process, product, or practice that you could talk about as a group.

- Are there specific areas where your managers are struggling? Could you offer some training or leadership development in those areas? You can bring in an outside trainer to teach specific skills like effective communication, delegation, accountability, etc.

- Do your managers understand and connect with the core elements of your strategy? You might need to use some of this time to bring your BFHAG (Big Fat Hairy Audacious Goal) to life for your managers and help ignite passion for your long-term strategy.

- Does your team have difficulty working well together? You might consider going off site to do an activity together to help the team bond. You could also bring in a facilitator to do a DISC analysis for your team and help you find ways to work better together and communicate more effectively.

5. Wrap up the meeting. To do this effectively, you want to be sure to document any follow up items that came out of the discussion. You also want to be sure to close

by checking in with each person around the room, getting them to share a key takeaway from the meeting.

5.8 Business Budgets

You have a pre-agreed business budget for specific profit goals?

Every successful business needs a budget, and here are some tips on how to make one that works for you.

It's a basic principle of business - before you can make money you have to figure out how to spend it. Drafting a budget is a keyway to help you turn your dreams for business success into reality.

Using this vital tool, you can track cash on hand, business expenses, and now much revenue you need to keep your business growing - or at least afloat. By committing these numbers to paper, your chances of succeeding with your business are helped by anticipating future needs, spending, profits, and cash flow. It also may let you spot problems before they mushroom, so that you can switch gears.

It's like a roadmap for your company. You need the roadmap to understand where you're going with your business and determine how long it's going to take you to get there.

Conversely, if you don't have the discipline to sit down and assemble a business budget, you may not have insight into how your business is performing from year to year, whether there are cuts you can make to improve performance and whether you have the needed funds to purchase new equipment -- be it computers, trucks, machinery, or a new factory. "It's like being in a car without a map or GPS system," Butcher says. "You hope going in the right direction, but you don't know."

The following will detail why your business needs a budget, what components you should include in a budget, and how to get started drafting a budget, and how to use the budget to better your business performance.

Why Your Business Needs a Budget

The bottom line on why to draft a budget for your business is that it will help you figure out how much money you have, how much you need to spend, and how much you need to bring in to meet business goals. But there are other reasons, too. Bankers and other financiers may want to see a budget when you ask for a loan. Employees should also be privy to the budget so that they understand where the business is going and are motivated to work harder.

"It would be stupid not to share this with employees. Everybody should know what the goal of the company is. It's a group goal. Don't expect your staff to meet your goals if they don't know what they are."

Budgets can also help you minimize risk to your business. A budget should be created before you sign a new lease or invest in new machinery or equipment. It's better to find out that you can't afford new office space before you commit to spending a certain amount of money every month.

A budget can be used to indicate some of the following:

- The funds needed for labour and/or materials
- For a new business, total start-up costs
- Your costs of operations
- The revenues necessary to support the business
- A realistic estimate of expected profits

You can use this information to adjust your plans or expectations going forward.

A 12-month budget can be updated with actual expenditures and revenues each month so that you know you're on target. If you're missing the targets set out in your budget, you can use the budget to troubleshoot by figuring out how you can reduce expenses like labour or new computers, increase sales by more aggressive marketing, or lowering your profit expectations.

Components of a Budget

A budget should include your revenues, your costs, and - most importantly, your profits or cash flow so that you can figure out whether you have any money left over for capital improvements or capital expenses. A budget should be tabulated at least yearly. Most yearly budgets are also divided up into 12 months, with blank columns next to your estimates to fill in with your actual results as the year progresses. You may want to consult an accountant in preparing a budget, but it also may be something you can do yourself with small business financial software and/or some of the free budget worksheets and templates available online.

The basic budgeting components:

1. Sales and other revenues: These figures are a budget's "cornerstone." Try to make these estimates as accurate as possible, but always side on being conservative if you must. The best basis for your projected sales revenues are last year's actual sales figures. If you're just starting out, hopefully you have done your research by asking other businesspeople in the same field as you, using knowledge of the field you had at a previous job, and/or doing market research.

2. Total costs and expenses: Now that you have your sales estimates done, you can come up with figures for how much it will cost your business to earn those revenues. These can be tricky because sometimes they will vary because of inflation, price increases, and other factors.

Costs can be divided into categories: fixed, variable, and semi-variable.

- Fixed costs are those expenses that remain the same, whether your sales rise or fall. Some examples include rent, leased furniture, and insurance.
- Variable costs correlate with sales volumes. These include the cost of raw materials you need to make products, inventory, and freight.
- Semi-variable costs are fixed costs that can be variable when influenced by volume of business. These can include salaries, telecommunications, and advertising.

3. Profits: You are in business to make a profit on your investment and work. You estimate this figure by subtracting your costs from your revenues. Check with trade associations, accountants, or bankers to make sure that you're getting an appropriate profit from your business. Once you have profit estimates, you can also start to plan for whether you can purchase new equipment, move to a bigger location, add staff, or give your employees bonuses or raises. You can also troubleshoot your projected costs and see where you can cut if your profit projections aren't up to snuff.

The budget should operate according to basic mathematical equations -- either "sales = total cost + profit" or "sales - total cost = profit."

How to Draft a Business Budget

Drafting a budget is easiest if you wrote one the previous year. Those projections, coupled with the actual income and expense figures you realized, would form the basis of your estimates for the coming year. But if you're reading this article, the odds are that you've never written a budget for your business before. In that case, read on.

Target your sales and profits

Start out by developing a target for your sales revenues. For a start-up business, begin by estimating what type of realistic profit you'd like to see in the coming year. If you have been in business for a while, take your company's most recent financial statements - be they generated by a ledger or a computer software program - and use those as the basis for developing your sales and profit targets. The reason you start with sales and/or profits is because this information will drive the rest of your estimates for costs, expenses, and capital expenditures.

Take into considering factors that might affect your sales numbers - such as the economy or the loss of a major customer – but don't worry too much because the basic principle of budgeting is that the figures will never turn out to be exactly right.

Calculate operating expenses

A good place to start, once again, is those financial statements. These statements should include an itemized list of the fixed and variable expenses you incurred during the year, including salaries and wages, rent, postage, research, travel, utilities, taxes, etc. If you're just starting out, you're going to have to brainstorm to make sure you factor in all the costs you will incur.

Figure out gross profit margin

Again, this is much easier if you've been in business for a while. In that case, estimate the cost of your goods sold (beginning inventory, goods purchased or manufactured, shipping charges, etc.) and subtract that from your overall sales revenue.

Take time to re-adjust figures

Given the estimations for sales and expenses, you most likely will want to go back and readjust your estimates to reach your profit targets. This may mean you purchase fewer new supplies in the coming year, or you need to add two new employees. Factor in these adjusted costs and or savings and run the numbers again. You may need to bite the bullet and go to an accountant or business consultant for help with your budget figures. Either way, remember that it's important to use realistic figures so that your budget can help you guide your business. Remember that budgeting is not an exact science.

A budget works on common sense. If you made £100,000 last year in revenue, common sense indicates you won't make a million next year. Your best-off estimating in the range of £80,000 to £120,000.

But be prepared to adjust your budget as the year progresses. You may have set your sales figures too high when an economic slump hits your business. Or, conversely, you may land a client that doubles your business.

5.9 Pricing models

You regularly test different pricing models and margin strategies?

You can have the best product or service in the world, but if you don't have a solid and contextually based go-to-market (GTM) strategy and execution plan, you will fail. Marketing plays the critical role in building brand awareness, lead generation, prospect, and customer nurturing.

Business schools and countless business books discuss the importance of the 4 Ps (Product, Place, Price, and Promotion) as the key components to a solid marketing approach.

While all four Ps are important to a founding team's marketing strategy, the "P" I get asked the most about is pricing. Pick the right pricing model and you can transform your goals from concept to reality. Chose the wrong pricing strategy and you risk immediate failure.

Creating the right pricing strategy can be agonizing. It is a complex process that brings out insecurities in the best of us.

Your 5-step process to help you along the way:

1. Determine your business goals. How you make money determines everything about your marketing and sales GTM strategy.

These are the things you MUST consider when setting a pricing strategy:

- Increase profitability
- Improve cash flow
- Market penetration
- Larger market share
- Increase revenue per customer

- Beat the competition
- Fill capacity and utilize resources
- New product introduction
- Reach a new segment
- Increase prospect presence
- Increase prospect conversion

2. Conduct a thorough market pricing analysis. While the first step is grounded in your business goals, this step ensures that your pricing strategy considers the context of the market in which your product or service will compete.

Low-cost providers like Asda often market to a broad audience. Whilst high-cost providers like Tesla market to a super specific audience.

If your market and product are broader with many players who offer related products or services, chances are you will compete on price. You will need to do everything to keep operational costs down to ensure a maximum profits margin. Conversely, if you have a high value, highly differentiated product or service, your offering may be more conducive to premium pricing, which lends itself to a different form of targeted marketing. With a superior product, it is important that you can place emphasis on high quality marketing and customer service, and this is reflected through EVERYTHING about the business not just the sales tag.

3. Analyse your target audience. This step enables you to answer why, what, and how customers will use your product or service based on their specific and urgent needs.

Be guided by the most important questions:

- what perceived and real value does my product or service bring to the customer.
- What is the task they are facing?
- How does my product or service ease the pain associated with this task?
- What does my customer have to gain by using my product or service?

Your pricing model and promotional campaigns must align with why your customer would buy your product. For example, if you have a best-of-breed product that uniquely fulfils a customer's urgent needs, value-based premium pricing may be the best strategy. Creating low-cost promotions and giveaways will confuse your customers, undercut your value, and shrink your profit margin.

4. Profile your competitive landscape. Whether you are a low-cost provider or a differentiated seller, the pricing model and price point of your competitors is a significant pricing strategy influencer. Therefore, consider the following approach for direct and indirect competitors:

    - Identify at least three direct competitors. Study the structure of their pricing. For example, do they have component pricing and allow for heavy discounts? Do they bundle with other products or solutions? Or do they employ value-based pricing where clients pay a percentage of the total perceived ROI.
    - Consider the substitutes a customer may use to solve the task or problem that your product or service addresses. Find out how much these indirect competitors cost the customer. And remember, sometimes your indirect competitor is the word "no".

Consider of self-solutions, or no resolution, as well as other indirect vendor alternatives.

5. Create a pricing strategy and execution plan. At this point, you have gathered enough information to formulate an action plan. I've identified 10 pricing strategies to consider based on your market, customer, and competitive analysis:

   - **Penetration pricing**: Price is artificially low to break into the market
   - **Economy pricing**: Everyday low price with the focus on low manufacturing/delivery cost
   - **Premium pricing**: High price for high value
   - **Price skimming**: Go into the market with a high price, but once your competitors follow, lower your cost, and implement other pricing strategies
   - **Promotional pricing**: Discounts over a period, one-time deals
   - **Psychological pricing**: Price products or services which triggers action. For example, charging .99 instead of £1.00
   - **Versioning**: Offer different tiers for your services or products: good, better, best
   - **Sandwich pricing**: High-, medium- and low-priced item with the intent to drive customers to the medium-priced item
   - **Competitive pricing**: Set the price equal to what your competitors are charging and win the service game
   - **Value pricing**: Understand the value for your customers and their willingness to pay. Also understand what alternatives do they have?

After you have completed the five steps, take the time to work the steps backwards. This will help you ensure that the GTM actions you chose to take give you the best shot at successfully competing in your target market segments, gaining revenue and market share.

5.10 Financial Monitoring

You are using online financial systems to monitor your financials from outside your business?

Amy Harris and Hannah McIntyre didn't set out to start CrunchBoards. In fact, they were already running a business together when they came up with the idea. They were using Xero for their accounting and a combination of spreadsheets and other tools to do their forecasting and reporting.

Frustrated with the amount of admin time it took to get what they needed from their spreadsheets; they developed tools to give them the real-time, real-life forecasting they were looking for. When they realized what they'd created would work for all small businesses, CrunchBoards was born.

Think local, but launch global

By plugging into an already booming ecosystem, they were spared some of the typical growing pains and time delays. Instead, they could place greater focus interacting with the small businesses and the Xero community to refine their product and their customer service.

Xero crunchboards

They launched as a global add-on from day one and had leads coming straight from the Xero community (yet another reason to leverage networks when you launch).

Referrals are one of the most credible forms of marketing, and the online community made this even more viral. They had new enquiries filtering in from Boston to Kilkenny. Potential customers were exploring CrunchBoards based on what they'd heard. This led to a growth not possible if they had launched on their own. Building brand exposure as a new player can be expensive without a focused channel to support your growth.

KashFlow is a cloud-based accounting solution that caters to businesses of all sizes. Features include invoicing, estimation, credit control, accounting, purchase management, payroll, and reporting. Users can create invoices and receive email alerts when a payment is due.

Xero connects you to all things business. Its online accounting software connects you to accountants and bookkeepers, your bank, and a huge range of other business services and Apps. Xero is great for start-ups and those with limited knowledge where up to date, ease of access and mobile connectivity of key importance. There are several other cloud-based accountancy solutions, including things such as QuickBooks ZohoBooks, FreshBooks and probably the most well-known and well established the world over SAGE.

Sage 50 is better suited to more complex businesses with a stronger financial knowledge. They have been around a long time, have an international reputation, and although were a little late to come to the online cloud-based solution market, have an exceptional pedigree background, often considered the GOLD STANDARD within this industry.

Whichever option you choose, I simply say choose one. In such a digital world we now operate in (and with Her Majesties Revenue & Customs) now insisting on Digital Returns, you MUST operate a cloud-based system to get the level of reporting as easily and up to date as required in a 24/7 business.

5.11 Financial Management

You have a Finance Manager in place.

A dashboard is a financial reporting tool used for quick visual comparative analysis of key performance indicator data, often in the form of a series of side-by-side trend diagrams. Dashboards can distil a great deal of data on and visually summarize a wide variety of results on a single page.

How To Build Your Financial Dashboard

The first thing that usually comes to mind is a financial dashboard. When you create a dashboard that gives an effective overview of your fiscal performance, you have a powerful tool in your hands to make smart decisions. Your leadership team will know what's profitable and what's not, in addition to lots of other "pounds and Pence" data.

1. **Figure out your goals**

If you use a Balanced Scorecard, the goals or objectives from the financial perspective would be a great place to start building your dashboard. This perspective is usually straightforward and tracks your profits, revenue,

and costs. Most of the measures in this perspective are lagging indicators because they tell you what happened last month or last quarter.

2. **Decide which metrics to include**

Your dashboard should display metrics that provide a broad view of your company's financial health. These vary by organization, but it's common to see numbers related to profit, cash flow, revenue, etc. Two important things to keep in mind when choosing your dashboard metrics:

- Don't display an overwhelming amount of data. Keep it high-level, while offering the ability to drill down into details if needed.
- Summarize and interpret the numbers, versus just reporting them.

When you're thinking about the metrics to include, also consider the audience. Ask yourself: Who will be viewing this dashboard? What numbers do they care about? Where will this be published?

For example, if you're a non-profit, you'll likely have one version of a financial dashboard posted on your website showing how donations or taxes are spent in a format that's easily understood by the public. You'll have a second version of the dashboard containing more detailed, confidential numbers and "insider information" suited for the eyes of senior stakeholders. Plus, if those stakeholders happen to be CFOs, then maybe it's appropriate to use complex ratios or advanced scoring.

3. Track and report performance

As a barometer of financial health, a dashboard should report on your organization's performance. Depending on the measures you use in your dashboard, some may be more suited to revealing trends over time while others may simply tell a story for that accounting period. For example, revenue and net income are ideal to track over time to understand important trends. In contrast, something like a ratio may be best displayed with other ratios for the current period only to indicate performance.

Revenue over time

You should also have targets for your measures. With targets, you can see if you are above or below your plan. This will tell viewers where you're succeeding and where you may be struggling so you can make informed strategic decisions. Many organizations use Red, Amber, and Green status indicators

(RAG status) to quickly tell readers if this measure is above or below plan.

4. Chart it

Charts are exceptional visual aids, and we strongly recommend using them in your financial performance dashboards. It's easier for viewers to understand metrics if they are displayed graphically, versus simply writing about how an objective is performing. Here are a few best practices to follow:

- For single data points, display the status in some way (such as a RAG status).
- If a metric is cyclical, show year-over-year (YOY) performance. For some industries—retail for example—it's more helpful to compare performance YOY than against the previous month.
- If it's beneficial to combine multiple metrics, do that! For example, short-term assets for cash, investments, and A/R should all be plotted together.

Short-term assets

Try to use similar charts for all measures. If you design a new chart for each measure, then the reader must first figure out the chart, then figure out the data. For example, it's easier to know that "Actual" results are a blue bar and "Target" results are a red line for all measures.

5. Determine frequency

We recommend generating strategic dashboards on a quarterly basis. Anything more frequent than that cadence will turn into detailed operational measures and metrics. There's nothing wrong with an operational dashboard, but it will most likely be suited for the financial operations team versus the

strategic or executive teams. For high-level, strategic financial dashboards, quarterly is best.

After you build your financial performance dashboard, keep these three things in mind:

- Don't get hung up on perfecting your dashboard right out of the gate. Accept that it's a work in progress. Get a version in front of stakeholders and gather feedback so you can gradually tweak it until you reach perfection.
- Identify a person or team to own and manage the dashboard. There should be a single source "controlling" the contents and distribution.
- In addition to making sure all data gets added to the dashboard at the designated frequency, review and verify the data each reporting period. It's critical that it remains accurate and relevant.

Remember that your strategic plan and success shouldn't be solely focused on your financial metrics—the Balanced Scorecard framework includes three other perspectives. Operations, customers, and the people who make up your organization are all important, too, and will have their own metrics and dashboards.

There are a few fabulous books I highly recommend for anyone wanting to gain further understanding about the information shared within this chapter.

Living on the fault line *by Geoffrey A. Moore*

The fault line - that dangerous, unstable seam in the economy where the Internet and other powerful innovations meet and create market-shattering tremors. Every company lives on it; no manager can control it. Everyone must learn to deal with it.

Geoffrey Moore explores the new management paradigms that will guide businesses in the twenty-first century how to survive and thrive on the fault line.

The art of profitability *by Adrian Slywotzky*

An extraordinarily new business slant on how companies can generate greater profits. Presented in 23 compact lessons, "The Art of Profitability" features an ongoing tutorial between two fictitious individuals.

"Your life, your legacy" *by Roger J. Hamilton* in which he covers all about the Legacy you leave behind and how working towards a Legacy has such a profound impact on both you, your decision making and the outcomes within both your personal and business life.

"Money: Master the game, 7 simple steps to financial freedom" *by none other than Anthony Robbins.*

Who needs no further introduction, other than to say: read it!

This alongside **"Money"** *by my good friend Rob Moore,* are by far two great books I've read on the importance of understanding money, what it is, how to generate it, what to do with it and how it works!

Chapter Six:

Sales & Negotiation

6.6 End Goals

You know your end goal & have a matrix to measure performance towards it?

I'm not sure how many times I've advised people to start with the end in mind! It's many, and yet so few do this when they start in business or if they do, it's a notional consideration rather than doing the research, the hard work, dotting the I's and crossing the t's and actually knowing the date, the amount, who, where when and why the exit goes through and what to do next!

I cannot urge you strongly enough to take a DAY out of your business, and plot what EXIT looks like. Give it some REAL consideration (as if it were about to happen) and work on determining EVERY aspect of both the exit and what you want to do next.

Get real. Get numbers (accurate not assumptive) and PLOT the ongoing sale of the business. Ask yourself:

- When are you going to exit?
- How much do you want to exit with?
- Who will buy the business for that?
- Why will they pay that for it?

Determine what the business needs to look like in terms of sales, sales pipeline, staff, products/services provided, to who, when, for how much in return? Get REAL about the sale of the business.

Now come back to the here and now and establish how far away are you from those figures? I'm not asking you to sell tomorrow, but I am telling you, until you start to think about the legacy of the business, its future potential growth (beyond your involvement with it) it is unlikely to have one. Like everything in business, YOU must make it happen. So, get busy and determine what the future business organisation structure looks like? What products and services you provide to whom, and why they buy from you. Then establish how many of them do you need to sell, to hit YOUR exit figure?

6.7 Conversion Tracking

You track your conversions by:

| **Lead source** |
| **New Customers** |
| **Existing Customers** |

Tracking conversions is one thing but understanding where they come from. And not just at a superficial level of X referred Y. But really drilling down to where X came from, how X came to know of, and operate in this referring capacity? What is the journey X has taken to become a referrer. Really helps understand WHERE our leads and conversions come from. It might have been a call that the salesperson converted to a sale. But what other touch points has that prospect already had prior to the call. On average a new customer converts after 7-15 touch points! Each one of them taking them closer to the sale, but not actually making the sale. Yet take any one of them away, the chain is broken and potentially the sale would never have come through.

6.8 Sales Meeting

You have weekly/monthly sales meetings?

You have probably gathered by now. The bigger the business becomes, the more your time will be kept busy with meetings! Sales are the life blood of the business, and so regular meetings to learn, share, understand, gain feedback regarding current sales performance is crucial to not missing opportunity by failing to react to market demands.

Not only do regular sales meetings keep you informed, but they also give the sales team a weekly target (driven by accountability) to work towards every day.

6.9 Nurture Sequencing

You have automated nurture & rapport systems in place for warm leads?

So, you've launched an inbound campaign and started to attract good leads. That's great, but it's just the start. Now you must keep those leads happy, while gently leading them through the buyer's journey to sales-ready qualification. If your sales cycle is a long one that's not always easy.

Sending leads inappropriate content and interrupting them with unsolicited sales calls is increasingly ineffective. Instead, to increase close rates, avoid wasted sales time and reduce the sales cycle, leads should be nurtured with appropriate content to ensure they understand the value of your solution before sales teams contact them.

Many marketers may think they already run effective lead nurture campaigns. But using automated lead nurture as part of an inbound campaign ensures all leads get quick responses and are automatically sent the right content for them. No lead is forgotten, and no content wasted.

Challenges of Long Sales Cycles

50% of qualified leads aren't ready to buy. They might be open to education and delighted that you can identify their pain points. But, signing up for your solution? They're not there yet, and may not be for a while, depending on the length of your sales cycle.

That means sectors with long sales cycles, such as the SaaS and software industries, which have an average cycle of 3-18 months (and there's some suggestion that B2B sales cycles are getting longer across the board), face huge challenges in keeping leads interested and moving them smoothly through the sales funnel.

They might lack appropriate content to last the length of the sales cycle, or simply fail to notice leads wandering off the path. Equally, they might bore leads with repeat content, or lose them in bottlenecks.

The upshot can be lost leads and a lot of wasted effort by both marketers and sales teams. The wrong content discourages leads from moving along the sales path. Sales teams engage with leads at inopportune moments, wasting everybody's time.

Automated lead nurturing tackles these challenges

What is Automated Lead Nurturing?

We know that lead nurturing works but traditionally, nurture is labour intensive. The average buyer's journey is complex, and the content that helps move them through the sales funnel from awareness (of a problem) to consideration (of solutions), to decision (of what solution to buy) needs to be expertly honed and perfectly timed.

Random one-off emails to your database won't cut it in a competitive world, especially during a long sales cycle. Talking up the detailed benefits of your solution to someone who is only vaguely aware of a problem is pointless at best. By the same token, emailing simplified educational material to a highly educated lead desperately seeking a solution is potentially counterproductive.

Automating lead nurturing, on the other hand, allows for the systematic tracking of lead engagements with your content and site, and accurate pinpointing of that lead's stage in the sales cycle. That means you can drip feed appropriate content at the right time – leads are never forgotten, and opportunities never missed.

Companies who excel at lead nurturing generate 50% more sales ready leads at 33% lower cost. Automated lead nurturing, done properly, is the gold standard in its field.

The 3 Pillars of Automated Lead Nurturing

Many marketers already automate some of the nurturing process, but it is the combination of three key points that make automated lead nurturing especially powerful.

1. Nurturing. You likely do this already and send your leads content, from blog posts to infographics to case studies. But according to Pardot's State of Demand Generation study, 77% of buyers want different content at each stage of their research. Targeting your content formats and focusing on the lead's buyer's journey stage is vital and creating automated email workflows makes the process easier.

2. Segmentation. When leads interact with your content, tracking their responses in detail allows for segmentation. Leads are divided into appropriate contact lists, likely by niche or pain point. Without an automated workflow, the next round of emails would be adjusted manually. But with an automated process, emails can be drip-fed to designated contact lists, delivering relevant information at the right time.

3. Grading. Marketing automation lets you pinpoint exactly where a lead is in the sales cycle, so your contact lists – and the content sent to them – is constantly refined and updated. Contact lists can be divided and subdivided again, targeting content with pinpoint accuracy. Grading leads based on their interactions with all marketing efforts allows you to move them smoothly through the sales funnel. When they reach a designated threshold (based on

a points total) suggesting sales-ready status then – and only then – are they passed to sales.

3 Ways Automated Lead Nurturing Supercharges Your Sales Cycle

At its simplest, automating the sales process means being able to track and use a lot more data than would otherwise be possible and use that information to more accurately segment and target leads, speeding their path through the sales funnel.

Your sales team don't waste time educating leads about your product and service. A fine-tuned nurturing machine means leads are informed already and won't have been passed to sales if they haven't been nurtured through to the decision stage.

At the outset, automated lead nurturing takes time to set up. You need to create relevant content to support your segmented workflows, set contact frequencies and make sure you have a lead grading system to move leads from one stage in the process to another. But once your campaign is established, it will continue to work for you, and give your marketing and sales teams time for other tasks.

Automation means bottlenecks are quickly identified and easily rectified. Automatic reporting can show where in the funnel leads are getting stuck, and it allows you to develop your content accordingly. In a nutshell, content is continually honed to address sales barriers and smooth the path to purchase.

If you haven't automated your lead nurturing process there's every chance your sales team are wasting time on leads that aren't sales ready, while irritating potential customers with mistimed and irrelevant contact.

Automated nurturing gently leads your targets through the sales funnel, breaking down barriers to sales with timely, appropriate content. The result? Your sales team spend far more time on sales-ready leads, supercharging your sales cycle.

6.10 Sales Team

You have automated sales funnels in place which are monitored weekly?

We live in the sparkly, shiny world of automation. Everything from switching lights on/off to assembling cars can now be automated. This calls for the question though—how important is automation? Is it really of much help?

The answer is yes. Automation is adding value by reducing manual labour, saving time, and in some cases, saving lives.

In a recent incident, the autopilot feature a Tesla alerted the driver awake when it detected that he had fallen asleep. Thanks to the automation amalgamation, his life was saved.

Automation has created a paradigm shift in the way we work, across industries and businesses. And it is the same in the case of sales. The daily life of a sales rep is a list of crucial tasks that can make or break a deal. These include sending out emails, making calls, creating contracts, negotiating deals and more. They do these tasks multiple times in a day for multiple accounts, and it might be challenging to stay on top of all the accounts with just manual work.

A Forrester report states that automating tasks can help save 90% of costs. You can increase efficiency and productivity while cutting down on costs. Those are enough reasons to invest in sales process automation. But how do you go about automating the sales process? Where do you start? Here are the five aspects of your sales process that can be automated:

1. Email

Studies say sales reps spend 21% of their day on emails. That is a large chunk of their day, almost a quarter, which can be better spent talking to prospects. This calls on the urgent need for email automation.

To get started with email automation, you need to analyse the daily sales tasks performed by your sales reps and figure out:

- What are the most common emails that are sent daily?
- What is the time spent on creating and editing emails before hitting send?
- How much personalization and customization are needed for each email?

There are quite a lot of sales emails being sent in a day, and many are repetitive. As part of the sales cycle, sales reps send out various generic emails like:

- Welcome emails to new leads
- Follow up emails to unresponsive leads
- Demo emails to new sign ups
- Reminder emails about meetings
- Thank you emails to new customers

Creating the email copy, customizing it for each lead and sending them out requires a good chunk of your sales rep's time. Let's assume that a follow up email containing a helpful resource needs two minutes of preparation time before hitting send. If the sales rep must send the email to 10 other prospects, that is 20 minutes of their time. Also, these emails are only the first touch point in the sales process. They need to spend more time on highly personalized emails for nurturing the leads further. These would take more time to prepare and send, and your sales reps would end up spending hours just sending out nurture emails.

Your frustrated sales reps deserve better, and email templates can eliminate this frustration. Rather than typing out the same email repeatedly, they can create and save email templates that can be repurposed as needed saving tons of time. They can also schedule emails so that they can be sent out to multiple prospects at the same time.

However, not all emails can be automated. Sales reps exchange multiple emails with prospects, customers, and team members and these need to be manually worked on. Some emails require personalization based on content and context. Email automation cannot come into play for emails containing:

- Discussion on legal parameters
- Pricing negotiations
- Questions on premium features of the product
- Confirming meetings
- Contacting a C-level executive

DO'S: When creating emails templates, keep in mind to customize email signatures with links to collateral that can further help nurture the lead.

For example, in a "thank you for signing up" email, add links to product videos and customer case studies. This would help the lead understand product features and use cases better.

Always add a hint of customization to bulk emails using placeholders.

DON'TS: Avoid sending emails during their out of office hours. Schedule emails according to the time zone of the recipient.

2. Lead Prioritization

Your business may receive a high volume of leads from multiple resources. Some of these leads may be looking for a fling while some may be interested in starting a relationship with your company. While it makes no sense to spend a lot of time with the former set of leads, your sales reps may not be aware of that. There are, of course, AI-based lead scoring tools to help your sales reps prioritize leads. But before you go ahead and get one for your business, ask yourself the following questions.

- Are your sales reps spending a big chunk of their time in the qualification process?
- Are the conversion rates low?
- Are your sales cycles longer due to leaks and bottlenecks?

If the answer is yes to any of the questions, your business can benefit from automating the lead prioritization process.

Before you set off to create your lead scoring model, consider the metrics that are indicative of your business type. Most businesses score leads based on explicit signals like job title, industry type and company size. In some cases, businesses require deeper knowledge into how the customer uses the product and can lead based on implicit signals like website activity, page visits, and collateral downloaded.

Depending on how your customer uses the product, you can create a hybrid scoring system, using a mix of implicit and explicit signals. For instance, you can grant a higher score to a CFO who visits the pricing page as compared to an intern who visits the landing page.

DO'S: If you are a multi-product company, set up different lead scoring models for each product. Set thresholds for the scores on the lead and bucket your leads based on their score as cold, warm, and hot.

DON'TS: Make sure you configure the model for negative scoring. This is a common mistake made while creating lead scoring models. We consider only positive attributes but over time, the lead interest may begin to wane. For instance, you can assign negative scores to leads who have stopped engaging with your website and aren't responding to the emails sent by the sales rep.

Do not score based on vanity metrics like say, email opens. They are not the best indicators of the lead's interest as the lead may have opened the email multiple times to read it but may not have gotten the chance.

3. Lead distribution

Research indicates that calling a lead within the first five minutes of sign up will increase the likelihood of them answering the call by 100X. But this isn't the case in most companies. In most cases, the business receives leads from multiple sources—website, blog, and social media—and they remain untouched within the CRM for a period before being assigned to a sales rep. There is a gap in the time from when the lead enters the CRM, and the sales rep reaches out to them.

This is where lead distribution comes in. By automating lead assignment, the response time is cut down which, in turn, increases the lead conversion ratio. You can assign leads by geography, industry type, company size, and deal value, making it a lot easier and faster for the sales rep to get in touch with prospects. This helps increase sales efficiency as it avoids multiple reps reaching out to the same lead.

DO'S: If you have leads from all over the globe or have a multi-product business, you can automatically assign leads to sales rep handling a particular region or product.

4. Day-to-day tasks

Apart from modular tasks like sending emails and qualifying leads, sales reps do various administrative tasks daily. These contribute in small ways to the larger growth of sales.

The various tasks could entail:

Data entry

The true success of a CRM lies in the fact that it serves as a sole source of truth. It is an organized collection of data on prospects, customers, deals, accounts, and related sales activities. But this information must be entered manually by the sales rep. Automating CRM data entry can help reduce the time and effort spent on it.

With automatic call logging, your sales reps can crush their daily sales call quota and not worry about missing adding calls to the CRM. The CRM will automatically log calls into the respective lead profiles.

With lead enrichment tools, the lead profile can be auto populated with relevant information like job title, industry, and company. This eliminates the need for the sales rep to manually research on the lead.

Creating appointments and setting reminders

To schedule a meeting with a lead, there is usually a flurry of emails sent back and forth with various time slots. Automating appointments using a tool like Calendly can eliminate this hassle. You can forward a link to your calendar with the available time slots and the lead can choose their preferred time slot. A calendar invite is sent to both parties automatically and a reminder email is triggered before the scheduled time.

Invoice generation

When a deal is won, the deal status must be updated within the CRM. The sales rep must switch over to the invoice generation tool and create and generate an invoice for the lead. This is time-consuming as they must switch between tools. Using automation, an invoice can be generated automatically when the deal status is updated to "Won."

5. Report generation

Reports are tiresome and boring but extremely important. As a sales manager, you are responsible for revenue targets. You need to be aware of how the sales pipeline is moving and measure the output of the sales process. The easiest way to do this is to maintain records of the sales activities.

But collating data manually would involve updating a spreadsheet after each task is done with a description, like the number of calls completed, the outcome of the call and call notes. For each KPI, you must maintain multiple records. That's a lot of manual data entry, tabulation, and graph generation. If you miss adding an activity to the list, you will end up with erroneous data. That's where reporting automation can help you.

Before you automate your report generation, make a list of all the reports you need and the KPIs you need to track:

- Annual sales report
- Quarterly sales report
- Sales calls reports
- Sales emails reports
- Team performance comparison

These are team reports. For individual rep reports, you'd have to track their KPIs like:

- Emails sent
- Calls completed
- Qualified leads
- Deals created
- Closed lost
- Closed won

By automating reports, you can eliminate the manual task of collecting, organizing, and analysing data. This further excludes inaccuracies that are borne out of human error. Multiple reports can be created easily by choosing the necessary parameters. Sales rep performance can be tracked by customizing reports with the KPIs that need to be tracked.

DO'S: Schedule individual reports so that the rep is aware of their performance and can tweak their activities accordingly.

DON'TS: Avoid keeping information to yourself. Make the reports accessible to the team so they have visibility into how the team performance is progressing.

Profitable Sales Sequencing

You concentrate efforts on selling products which are the most profitable?

Make a profit every day with the Profit First Formula

We see a lot of business owners who haven't yet mastered their cash flow and aren't sure if they've made any money until the end of the year. Even worse, sometimes they haven't made money, but by the time they realize that it's too late to correct. That's a stressful place to be, and it doesn't need to be that way.

I first came across the PROFIT FIRST process when reading the book of the same name by Mike Michalowicz. It's a well-written book that teaches business owners how to "transform any business from a cash-eating monster to a money-making machine." Profit First focuses on a cash flow management system that ensures you'll take a profit and get paid, no matter how small that income might be.

Putting profit first

Sales – Expenses = Profit. While it makes sense to cover your expenses first, there's no guarantee that you'll make a profit with this formula.

The Profit First Formula flips the equation, giving profit the focus, it deserves: Sales – Profit = Expenses. You might wonder what difference this really makes—isn't it just semantics? Kind of. But what Michalowicz is trying to highlight for you is more psychological than anything: you must approach your business thinking profit first, not profit last.

The profit first method

The goal of the Profit First Formula is to develop a system for building your business in a sustainable way that creates long term success. First you account for your profit, taxes, and your own pay, and then what's left over is what the company must spend on everything else.

We usually think of expenses (e.g., cost of material, rent, salaries, utilities) as unavoidable, when they can often be eliminated, avoided, or delayed. When you discipline yourself to set aside a percentage of revenue for profit and only spend what's left to cover your expenses, you're forcing yourself to spend more wisely.

Doing that can be uncomfortable. It might mean you have to delay some of your spending on growth in the short term, even when you want to keep pushing forward. But it also means that when you do encounter a great opportunity to grow your revenue and profits, you'll have the resources to invest in it without endangering your business. If you put every spare pound back into your business, you might think you're planting seeds for growth—but you're putting yourself at risk for a future crisis.

How to put the Profit First Formula to work

Create smaller spending buckets

The first step you need to take is to get more granular with how you allocate your cash by creating smaller spending buckets. To make this easier, you'll need to set up bank accounts based on the core functions of your business:

- Income/revenue account
- Profit account
- Operating expenses account
- Owner's pay account
- Tax account

In addition, you might need a few other accounts depending on your business and the goals you want to achieve. Most businesses can get started with these five accounts and build out from there.

Determine your CAPS and TAPS

This is more technical part of the system. Your Current Allocation Percentages (CAPS) show where your Real Revenue is being spent right now—what your business is buying day-to-day in its current format. This is often the most interesting part of putting the Profit First Formula into action, since most business owners rarely pay close attention to that information.

The Target Allocation Percentages (TAPS) detail where we want your Real Revenue to go once the business in running at efficiency and profitability. You won't hit these numbers overnight, or even this year in many cases, but you can't work towards them until you know what they are. It's important to note that depending on the size and nature of your business some of these numbers might deviate significantly from those outlined in the book.

Transfer your Cash

Establish a rhythm for transferring the funds that are accumulating in your income account to your other accounts. How often should that happen? It's completely up to you. Almost every business owner starts out thinking they need to follow to the 10/25 rhythm outlined in the book, but this isn't necessary. Some business owners do it every two weeks, while others do it weekly. But once you establish your rhythm you need to stick to it!

Make Payments

Use your profit first accounts to pay your bills. The key is to ensure that each account is only used for its designated purpose.

1. Profit account: This account accumulates a very small amount 'off the top' that can be used for debt reduction, emergencies and for you to receive a bonus for all your hard work. The Profit First Formula is about generating profit, so this account comes first!
2. Owner's pay: This account is used to pay your after-tax salary or wage. Fight the temptation to 're-invest' this into your business because it's your salary. You need to get paid!
3. Tax Account: Use this account to meet all your tax and superannuation obligations.

4. Operating Expenses: This is all the money your business has available for operating expenses. Get creative and spend it wisely because all the other accounts are spoken for.

Review

At the end of each quarter the system should be reviewed and adjusted. The Profit First mindset shift will challenge you to re-evaluate every element of your business model as well as your personal financial situation. As your situation changes, so too will your need for cash and your account transfers should reflect these changes.

6.12 You have a sales manager

Do you have a high-performance sales manager in place, capable of recruiting, training, and managing sales teams to consistently hit targets?

The Importance of Sales Managers and 4 Steps for How to Keep Them

Any scaling business has as much chance of succeeding without a sales manager as a football team without a head coach — zero chance, to be exact. Sales managers organize, orchestrate, motivate, calculate, and undertake a host of other activities that keep sales teams on goal and advancing in terms of revenue production and skill.

Great sales managers are hard to find and extremely valuable, but experience shows they tend to leave firms after two or three years. With companies struggling to maintain continuity in sales force leadership, here are four suggestions for how they can retain star sales managers' long term.

1. Don't Expect Sales Managers to Do Everything

Organizations must separate their sales manager "wish list" from their sales manager "reality list." Sure, it would be terrific to find a sales manager skilled in social selling, lead generation, recruiting, training, negotiating, closing, CRM management

and producing dynamic growth. Though in reality, finding a manager skilled in three or four of these areas, and giving him talented support in the other areas, is by far a more realistic formula for retaining sales managers. When they expect the impossible, organizations can expect the sales manager to fail.

2. Give Sales Managers Real Authority

Talented sales managers will never remain satisfied in a position where they lack the authority to make meaningful decisions. If a business owner or C-level executive is continually looking over the sales manager's shoulder for every personnel and policy decision that comes along, it won't be long before that sales manager is scouring job listings in search of a position with more independence. A better formula for retention: give sales managers autonomy and hold them accountable. It's a tougher path, but that's exactly what top sales managers crave.

3. Don't Let Sales Managers Work in a Vacuum

At the other extreme, some organizations are too "hands off" with sales managers, which also results in retention problems. For sales managers to be confident and successful, they need feedback, guidance, ongoing training, a career path and awareness of changing business dynamics and strategy. Without these things, the direction they give to the sales team will grow more and more out of focus — and ever less effective.

4. Make Goals Attainable — But Not Too Attainable

When sales managers receive impossible marching orders — that is, goals beyond human reach — they are demoralized immediately. Most companies are aware of this, but the other extreme, setting goals too easy to achieve, also lays the

foundation for a sales management revolving door. Top sales managers seek a challenge because meeting it gives them a sense of accomplishment.

Where Does Your Organization Stand?

High turnover in sales management is a serious issue. First, the cost of hiring and training new sales managers is significant. Second, turnover disrupts the entire sales team, dragging down new account and new business production. Finally, and perhaps most seriously, customers perceive sales manager turnover as a sign of instability and unreliability.

It all adds up to this: companies of all sizes benefit from viewing sales management as a long-term career rather than a short-term gig. Does your organization have the pieces in place to make it happen?

To sell is human - **The Surprising Truth About Moving Others** *by Daniel H. Pink*

Daniel H. Pink draws on a rich trove of social science for his counterintuitive insights.

Along the way, Pink describes the six successors to the elevator pitch, the three rules for understanding another's perspective, the five frames that can make your message clearer and more persuasive, and much more.

The psychology of Selling - Increase Your Sales Faster and Easier Than You Ever Thought Possible *by Brian Tracy*

More salespeople have become millionaires because of listening to and applying his ideas than from any other sales training process ever developed.

Go-givers sell more *by Bob Burg & John David Mann*

Go-Givers Sell More, a practical guide that makes giving the cornerstone of a powerful and effective approach to selling.

Drawing on a wide range of examples of real-life salespeople who have prospered by giving more, Burg and Mann offer tips and strategies that anyone in sales can start applying right away.

Chapter Seven:

Service & Delivery

7.5 Customer Profiling

You have profiled your top 20 customers to establish your IDEAL TARGET MARKET AVATAR

Time is your greatest asset; make sure you spend your time wisely on the accounts that are most likely to use your services. To do this, you must define your Ideal Customer Profile (ICP) to understand the specific types of companies for your sales team to pursue.

Defining your Ideal Customer Profile helps you to:

- Focus your sales and marketing efforts on the companies that are most likely to buy from you now.
- Sell to companies with the highest success potential of using your product or service. A customer that isn't a good fit for your service drains time from your Customer Success team and may end up costing your company more than can be gained from the partnership.
- Create smart short-lists of companies to focus on, track buying signals within these accounts, and act fast when a window of opportunity presents itself to you as a salesperson.

An Ideal Customer Profile is a model account whose characteristics indicate that they would gain significant value from your product or service and in turn, provide significant value to your company as well.

Basing your Customer Profile off a gut feeling leaves a lot of room for error in judgement. Using insights from open data in understanding who your Ideal Customer Profile is will minimize the risk of missing many of the less obvious indicators of accounts that you and your team should ideally target.

You have a lot to gain by reaching out to potential customers immediately when a new need occurs in the organization, if not before this need has even materialized.

As soon as you have a clear idea of the companies you should be targeting, track every important buying signal within these accounts, using these insights to increase the success rate of your efforts in sales and marketing.

There is no such thing as a "universal" Ideal Customer Profile

As with everything worth having – finding your Ideal Customer Profile takes work. There is no universal "Ideal Target Client" definition, not for any company. This set of defined criteria is constantly evolving, as different companies stand to gain value from your product or service at different intervals of time. Re-evaluate this description of your Ideal Customer Profile every 6-9 months to use your time more efficiently in sales.

7.6 Profit Mapping

You map the cost & profit of each product/service

In commerce, customer experience (CX) is the product of an interaction between an organization and a customer over the duration of their relationship.

This interaction is made up of three parts:

1. the customer journeys
2. the brand touchpoints the customer interacts with
3. and the environments the customer experiences (including digital environment) during their experience.

A good customer experience means that the individual's experience during all points of contact matches the individual's expectations.

Customer experience implies customer involvement at different levels – such as rational, emotional, sensorial, physical, and spiritual. Customers respond diversely to direct and indirect contact with a company. Direct contact usually occurs when the purchase or use is initiated by the customer. Indirect contact often involves advertising, news reports, unplanned encounters with sales representatives, word-of-mouth recommendations or criticisms.

Customer experience encompasses every aspect of a company's offering—the quality of customer care, but also advertising, packaging, product and service features, ease of use, and reliability. Creating direct relationships in the place where customers buy, use, and receive services by a business intended for customers such as instore or face to face contact with the customer which could be seen through interacting with the customer through the retail staff.

We then have indirect relationships which can take the form of unexpected interactions through a company's product representative, certain services or brands and positive recommendations – or it could even take the form of "criticism, advertising, news, reports" and many more along that line.

Customer experience is created by the contribution of not only the customers' values but also by the contribution of the company providing the experience.

All the events experienced by customers before and after a purchase are part of the customer experience. What a customer experiences are personal and may involve sensory, emotional, rational, and physical aspects to create a memorable experience. In the retail industry, both company and customers play a big role in creating a customer experience.

Forbes describes the customer experience as the "cumulative impact of multiple touchpoints" over the course of a customer's interaction with an organization. Some companies are known to segment the customer experience into interactions through the web and social media, while others define human interaction such as over-the-phone customer service or face-to-face retail service as the customer experience.

According to Forrester Research, the six disciplines for great customer experience are

1. strategy
2. customer understanding
3. design
4. measurement
5. governance
6. and culture

A company's ability to deliver an experience that sets it apart in the eyes of its customers will increase the amount of consumer spending with the company and inspire loyalty to its brand.

loyalty is now driven primarily by a company's interaction with its customers and how well it delivers on their wants and needs

In today's competitive climate, more than just competitive prices and innovative products/services are required to survive in business. Customer experience involves every point of contact you have with a customer and the interactions with the products or service of the business. Customer experience has emerged as a vital strategy for all businesses.

Businesses can create and modify touchpoints so that they are suited to their consumers which changes/enhances the customers' experience. Creating an experience for the customer can lead to greater brand loyalty and brand recognition in the form of logos, colour, smell, touch, taste, etc

Development

There are many elements in the shopping experience associated with a customer's experience. Customer service, a brand's ethical ideals and the shopping environment are examples of factors that effect a customer's experience. Understanding and effectively developing a positive customer experience has become a staple within businesses and brands to combat growing competition. Many consumers are well informed, they can easily compare two similar products or services together. Therefore, consumers are looking for experiences that fulfil their emotional and physical expectations. A brand that can provide these gains a competitive advantage over their competition.

Males and females both respond differently to brands and therefore, will experience the same brand differently. Males respond effectively to relational, behavioural, and cognitive experiences whereas females respond greater to behavioural, cognitive, and effective experiences in relation to branded apps.

Customer experience is not limited to the purchase alone. It includes all activities that may influence a customer's experience with a brand. An effective way to develop a positive customer experience is by actively engaging a customer with an activity. Human and physical components of an experience are very important. Customers can recall active, hands-on experiences much more effectively and accurately than passive activities. However, this can also have a negative effect on the customer's experience. Just as active, hands-on experiences can greatly develop value creation, it can also greatly facilitate value destruction. This is related to a customer's satisfaction of their experience.

By understanding what causes satisfaction or dissatisfaction of a customer's experience, management can appropriately implement changes within their approach.

Management

Customer experience management (CEM or CXM) is the process that companies use to oversee and track all interactions with a customer during their relationship. This involves the strategy of building around the needs of individual customers.

Companies realize that building great consumer experiences is a complex enterprise, involving strategy, integration of technology, orchestrating business models, brand management and CEO commitment.

The term 'Customer Experience Management' represents the discipline, methodology and/or process used to comprehensively manage a customer's cross-channel exposure, interaction and transaction with a company, product, brand, or service. Businesses must define and understand all dimensions of the customer experience to have long-term success.

Although 80% of businesses state that they offer a "great customer experience," this contrasts with the 8% of customers expressing satisfaction with their experience. For companies to meet the demands of providing an exceptional customer experience, they must be able to execute the "Three Ds":

1. **Designing** the correct incentive for the correctly identified consumer, offered in an enticing environment
2. **Delivery**: a company's ability to focus the entire team across various functions to deliver the proposed experience

3. **Development** ultimately determines a company's success, with an emphasis on developing consistency in execution

CEM has been recognized as the future of the customer service and sales industry. Companies are using this approach to anticipate customer needs and adopt the mindset of the customer.

CEM depicts a business strategy designed to manage the customer experience and gives benefits to both buyer and seller. CEM can be monitored through surveys, targeted studies, observational studies, or "voice of customer" research. It captures the instant response of the customer to its encounters with the brand or company. Customer surveys,

customer contact data, internal operations process and quality data, and employee input are all sources of "voice of customer" data that can be used to quantify the cost of inaction on customer experience issues.

The aim of CEM is to optimize the customer experience through gaining the loyalty of the current customers in a multi-channel environment and ensure they are completely satisfied. It is also to create advocates of their current customers with potential customers as a word-of-mouth form of marketing.

A good indicator of customer satisfaction is the Net Promoter Score (NPS). This indicates out of a score of ten if a customer would recommend a business to other people. With scores of nine and ten these people are called protractors and will recommend other to the given product but on the other end of the spectrum are detractors, those who give the score zero to six. Subtracting the detractors from the protractors gives the calculation of advocacy. Those businesses with higher scores are likely to be more successful and give a better customer experience.

7.7 Net Promoter Score

You know your Net Promoter Score® & work consistently to improve it

Definition

The Net Promoter Score is an index ranging from -100 to 100 that measures the willingness of customers to recommend a company's products or services to others. It is used as a proxy for gauging the customer's overall satisfaction with a company's product or service and the customer's loyalty to the brand.

Net Promoter Score Calculation

Customers are surveyed on one single question. They are asked to rate on an 11-point scale the likelihood of recommending the company or brand to a friend or colleague. "On a scale of 0 to 10, how likely are you to recommend this company's product or service to a friend or a colleague?" Based on their rating, customers are then classified in 3 categories: detractors, passives, and promoters.

DETRACTORS

'Detractors' gave a score lower or equal to 6. They are not particularly thrilled by the product or the service. They, with all likelihood, won't purchase again from the company, could potentially damage the company's reputation through negative word of mouth.

PASSIVES

'Passives' gave a score of 7 or 8. They are somewhat satisfied but could easily switch to a competitor's offering if given the opportunity. They probably wouldn't spread any negative word-of-mouth but are not enthusiastic enough about your products or services to promote them.

PROMOTERS

'Promoters' answered 9 or 10. They love the company's products and services. They are the repeat buyers, are the enthusiastic evangelist who recommends the company products and services to other potential buyers.

The Net Promoter Score (NPS) is determined by subtracting the percentage of customers who are detractors from the percentage who are promoters. What is generated is a score between -100 and 100 called the Net Promoter Score. At one end of the spectrum, if when surveyed, all the customers gave a score lower or equal to 6, this would lead to a NPS of -100. On the other end of the spectrum, if all the customers were answering the question with a 9 or 10, then the total Net Promoter Score would be 100.

7.8 Customer Experience

You have a system to monitor and improve your customer experience

A customer experience management system is technology that helps you manage your organisation's interactions with customers, both current and potential. The system should work with all your customer-facing touchpoints: organising, automating, and synchronising them so that you can service all your existing customers and respond quickly to issues and new business, all in **one** place.

A customer experience management system stores all your customers' information in one place, with real-time updates that are easy to share with your various teams.

You'll be able to see a history of your interactions with customers from their behaviour (such as purchase or contact) to how it made them feel (customer feedback), revealing where you got customer service right, and where you maybe got it wrong.

Surveys

A good customer experience management system should be able to track valuable customer feedback across all your customer. This is usually done using a survey engine – you present customer surveys at various touchpoints and pull the responses into your (Customer Experience) CX platform.

You should be able to send surveys through a variety of methods from web and SMS surveys all the way through to Interactive Voice Response (IVR) and live chat modules. And it doesn't have to be a long survey either – one or two questions as a particular touchpoint can still be enough to gather the feedback you need.

Customer Experience Dashboard

A customer experience management system will usually surface your customer feedback and CX data in the form of dashboards. These provide a single view of what's happening whether it's your NPS score or a real-time view of the key trends in customer feedback.

The most advanced systems offer customisable, role-based dashboards – these are great because not everyone in the organisation needs the same data, so they allow you to control who sees what. For example, your leadership team won't care about the latest comments from your website checkout survey, while call centre agents won't be interested in the NPS score for your retail stores.

By customising the data, you show to different roles, you're able to show people the metrics that matter most to them, so they know where they can make an impact. Providing everything to everybody on the other hand risks information overload and doesn't provide people with actionable insights.

Customer Response Management

The most successful organisations go a step further than simply collecting and analysing customer feedback and use their system to respond to customers directly.

This is generally known as a closed-loop system as is a great way to build stronger relationships with customers by responding directly to their feedback and can help prevent customer issues from becoming much bigger problems.

A CX platform that allows you to close the loop with customers allows you to do this in the same platform where you're collecting feedback and managing customer contacts so you can track customer feedback from the survey response all the way through to resolution.

Integration

Customer feedback isn't the only data your organisation has – what website analytics, CRM systems and even HR and finance data?

Most of these platforms have APIs which allow you to send the data to other systems too.

Being able to integrate them into your CX platform can be a huge benefit as you get better visibility of the customer experience and its impact on your business.

Take website analytics for example – you may see an increase in people abandoning their cart, but it's hard to identify why looking only at the analytics data. But combine it with customer feedback and you can drill down to see what customers are saying too, so you can quickly and easily see the impact.

With CRM systems, integrating your data is a great way to get a 'one customer' view – you can tie feedback to contact records and start to tie your CX metrics into operational metrics like win-rate and revenue to really understand the impact of your customer experience on the bottom line.

Analytics

Having data is one thing but knowing what to do with it is quite another. So, look for the analytics capability in a CX platform.

Most platforms will include some level of analytics – after all, few organisations have a team of data scientists ready and waiting – that will help you understand what the data means.

There are plenty of types of analysis too:

1. **Statistical analysis**
   From simply relating one variable to another (e.g., how is NPS affected by call waiting time?) to a multivariate regression that takes hundreds of competing variables and models the precise impact of each one
2. **Text analysis**
   This technology takes open text responses and automatically sorts and analyses them, so you don't have to wade through them all. There are different levels of sophistication here from those that identify topics to those that analyse sentiment too so you can see which topics are talked of positively or negatively to spot trends.

3. **Key driver analysis**

   Identifies key relationships to surface the most important drivers of a particular metric like NPS or revenue so you can see which areas to focus on

CX platforms that offer this as a built-in capability can help you go from raw data to valuable customer insights without hundreds of hours of manual work.

You have read: **The Zappos Experience** *Joseph A. Michelli*

"The Zappos Experience" takes you through - and beyond - the playful, offbeat company culture Zappos has become famous for. Michelli reveals what occurs behind the scenes at Zappos, showing how employees at all levels operate on a day-today basis while providing the "big picture" leadership methods that have earned the company $1 billion in annual gross sales during the last ten years - with almost no advertising.

The ultimate question 2.0b - How Net Promoter Companies Thrive in a Customer-Driven World *by Fred Reichheld, Rob Markey.*

Would you recommend us to a friend?
By asking customers this question, you identify detractors, who sully your firm's reputation and readily switch to competitors, and promoters, who generate good profits and true, sustainable growth.

Practical and insightful, The Ultimate Question 2.0 provides a blueprint for long-term growth and success.

Chapter Eight:
Winning Team
8.6 Effective Recruitment Process

You have an effective recruitment system?

Recruitment should incorporate the following steps:

Step 1 – Before you start looking

Step 2 – Preparing a job description and person profile

Step 3 – Finding candidates

Step 4 – Managing the application process

Step 5 – Selecting candidates

Step 6 – Making the appointment

Step 7 – Induction

1. Before you start looking

Put together information about the nature of the job, especially it is a position being created for the first time. Think about:

- The content (such as the tasks) making up the job
- The output required by the job holder (work hours, number of clients etc.)
- How it fits into the structure of the practice/organisation
- The skills and personal attributes needed to perform the role effectively.
- This analysis forms the basis of a job description and person specification.

2. Preparing a job description

A job description states the necessary and desirable criteria for selection.

Increasingly such specifications are based on a set of competencies identified as necessary for the performance of the job. Include:

- Skills, aptitude, knowledge, and experience
- Qualifications (which should be only those necessary to do the job – unless candidates are recruited based on future potential, for example graduates)
- Personal qualities relevant to the job, such as ability to work as part of a team.

3. Finding candidates

Internal methods:

- Staff referrals
- Succession planning
- Secondments

It is important not to forget the internal talent pool, especially in a larger practice. Providing opportunities for development and career progression is an important factor for employee retention and motivation

External methods

There are many options available for generating interest from individuals outside the organisation.

- Online recruitment
- Press advertising
- Networking
- Open days for the larger organisation

Advertising remains the most common means of attracting and recruiting. Advertisements should be clear and indicate the:

- requirements of the job
- necessary and the desirable criteria for job applicants (to limit the number of inappropriate applications received)
- job location
- reward package
- job tenure (for example, contract length)
- details of how to apply.

Advertisements should be genuine and relate to a job that exists. They should appeal to all sections of the community using positive visual images and wording.

4. Managing the application process

There are two main formats in which applications are likely to be received: the curriculum vitae (CV)/résumé or application. These can be submitted either on paper or electronically.

Application forms

Application forms allow information to be presented in a consistent format, and therefore make it easier to collect information from job applicants in a systematic way and assess objectively the candidate's suitability for the job.

CVs/résumés

CVs give candidates the opportunity to sell themselves in their own way and don't have the restrictions of fitting information into a form. However, some candidates include irrelevant material that makes them harder to assess consistently.

5. Selecting candidates

Selecting candidates involves two main processes: short listing and assessing applicants to decide who should be made a job offer.

Shortlisting depends on the number of candidates.

When deciding who to shortlist, it is helpful to draw up a list of criteria using the job specification and person profile. Each application can then be rated according to these standards, or a simple scoring system can be used.

Assessment

A range of different methods can be used to assess candidates. These vary in their reliability as a predictor of performance in the job and in their ease and expense to administer. Typical methods include:

- General interview
- Competency based interview
- Role play/demonstration
- Sample presentation (for jobs needing presenting skills)

6. Making the appointment

Contract

Offers of employment should always be made in writing. But it is important to be aware that an oral offer of employment made in an interview is as legally binding as a letter to the candidate.

References

A recruitment policy should state clearly how references will be used, when in the recruitment process, they will be taken up and what kind of references will be necessary (for example, from former employers). These rules should be applied consistently.

Other checks

Checks such as working with children or vulnerable adults, police checks, fit to work checks are necessary according to the job.

7. Induction

Induction is a critical part of the recruitment process, for both employer and new employee. An induction plan should include:

- A clear outline of the job/role requirements
- Orientation (physical) – describing where the facilities are
- Orientation (organisational) – showing how the employee fits into the team, along with details of the organisation's history, culture, and values
- Fair Work Information Statement

8.7 Effective Induction Process

This is not a comprehensive guide to hiring!

However, these steps are vital to hiring an employee. If you need a step-by-step process, consider using this checklist for success in hiring employees.

1. Define the Job Before Hiring an Employee

Hiring the right employee starts with a job analysis. The job analysis enables you to collect information about the duties, responsibilities, necessary skills, outcomes, and work environment of a particular job.

The information from the job analysis is fundamental to developing the job description for the new employee. The job description assists you to plan your recruiting strategy for hiring the right employee.

2. Plan Your Employee Recruiting Strategy

With the job description in hand, set up a recruiting planning meeting that involves the key employees hiring the new employee. The hiring manager is crucial to the planning. Your recruiting strategy is planned at this meeting, and the execution begins. Teams that have worked together frequently in hiring an employee can often complete this step via email.

3. Use a Checklist for Hiring an Employee

This checklist for hiring an employee will help you systematize your hiring process. Whether it's your first employee or one of many employees you are hiring, this checklist for hiring an employee enables you to keep track of your recruiting efforts.

The checklist for hiring an employee keeps your recruiting efforts on track and communicates progress to interested employees and the hiring manager.

4. Recruit the Right Candidates When Hiring an Employee

You can develop relationships with potential candidates long before you need them when hiring an employee. These ideas will also help you recruit a large pool of candidates when you have a current position available.

The more qualified candidates you can develop when hiring an employee, the more likely you will locate an eligible potential employee. Read on to discover the best ways to build your talent pool when hiring an employee.

5. Review Credentials and Applications Carefully

Reviewing resumes, cover letters, job applications, and job application letters starts with a well-written job description. Your bulleted list of the most qualified candidate's most desired characteristics was developed as part of the recruiting planning process.

Screen all applicants against this list of qualifications, skills, experience, and characteristics. You'll spend your time with your most qualified candidates when hiring an employee. And that is a good use of your time.

6. Pre-screen Your Candidates

The most crucial reason to pre-screen candidates when hiring an employee is to save time for the interviewing and selection committee. While a candidate may look good on paper, a pre-screening interview will tell you if their qualifications truly fit your job.

Additionally, in a pre-screening interview, you can determine whether their salary expectations are congruent with your job. A skilled telephone interviewer will also obtain evidence about whether the candidate may fit within your culture - or not.

7. Ask the Right Job Interview Questions

The job interview is a decisive factor in hiring an employee. The job interview is vital tool employers utilize in hiring. The job interview questions asked are critical in magnifying the power of the job interview to help you in hiring the right employee.

Interview questions that help you separate desirable candidates from average candidates are fundamental when hiring an employee. Job interview questions matter to employers. Here are sample job interview questions.

8. Check Backgrounds and References when Hiring an Employee

Adequate background checks are the most important steps when hiring an employee. It would help if you verified that your candidate possesses all the presented, sterling credentials, skills, and experience.

The background checks must include work references, especially former supervisors, educational credentials, employment references and actual jobs held, and criminal

history. Other background checks when hiring an employee, such as credit history, must be specifically related to the position you are hiring.

9. 7 Critical Factors to Consider Before Hiring an Employee

When you consider hiring an employee, it's tempting to offer the job to the candidate who is most like you. The candidate feels as comfortable as a well-worn shoe. You won't get many surprises once you make the job offer, and your gut is satisfied that your favourite candidate can do the job.

Beware, beware of this practice when hiring an employee. Why does your organization need another employee just like you? Here are the seven critical factors to consider before hiring an employee and making a job offer.

10. Extend a Job Offer

The job offer letter is provided to the candidate you have selected for the position. Most frequently, the candidate and the organization have verbally negotiated the conditions of hire, and the job offer letter confirms the verbal agreements about salary and benefits.

However, the more senior the position, the more likely the job offer will turn into a protracted negotiation about salary, benefits, employment termination, bonus potential, severance pay, stock options, and more when hiring an employee.

11. Use Effective Employment Letters When Hiring an Employee

These sample employment letters will assist you to reject job candidates, making job offers, welcoming employees, and more when hiring an employee. Use these sample employment letters to develop the employment letters you use in your organization when hiring an employee.

7 Qualities of a Good Employee

How can we define the qualities of a good employee? When separating the average worker from the best and brightest, what do employers look for? While every business will have its own unique needs, everyone seems to value some top employee characteristics.

Understanding these employee traits, and recognizing them in candidates, can help improve your recruitment process. Do your senior leaders value employees who are confident and self-motivated? You could assign applicants a task and see who takes the most initiative to go above and beyond the assignment.

CareerBuilder conducted a study with Harris Poll last year to better understand the typical qualities of a good employee that the average employer is looking for. They surveyed over 2,000 hiring managers and HR professionals on soft skills–those less tangible characteristics related more to personality than ability.

Some of the results may seem obvious (how many job descriptions don't call for an organised candidate?), but the most significant outcome was the importance of soft skills. More than three-quarters of respondents–77%–said soft skills are just as necessary as hard skills. An additional 16% described soft skills as more important than hard skills when evaluating candidates. Below are some of the specific qualities of a good employee hiring managers are after.

1. Strong work ethic: Setting and achieving goals

Tied in first place, a strong work ethic was one of the most popular qualities hiring managers look for in a candidate. According to CareerBuilder, 73% of respondents want to see applicants demonstrate their ability to work hard. Candidates

who set high goals for themselves, or respond well to stretch goals from supervisors, indicate a willingness to do more than clock in and clock out every day.

2. Dependable: Consistently following through

Also chosen by 73% of respondents, dependability can differentiate between a candidate who usually follows through and who always does. Candidates who are committed to completing tasks on time, as assigned, during the application process will likely continue this behaviour as employees.

3. Positive attitude: Creating a good environment

At a close third among respondents to the CareerBuilder survey (72%), a positive attitude has myriad benefits for individual employees and their colleagues. Positivity leads to a more productive workday and creates a better environment for fellow employees. Great employees consistently stand out for their upbeat attitudes and earn positive reputations. One trait to look for in a candidate is acknowledging mistakes and moving forward positively. This suggests they'll be equally resilient in the workplace.

4. Self-motivated: Working effectively with little direction

Two-thirds of respondents (66%) listed self-motivation as a critical soft skill among candidates. When it comes to finding good employees, hiring managers often look for candidates who can take the initiative and get work done with little to no encouragement. Sheer enthusiasm and interest in the work is usually enough to drive these employees. And this self-motivation goes hand in hand with confidence—chosen by 46% as a top soft skill among candidates.

5. Team-oriented: Making the most out of collaboration

Think about the great employees you already have. Do they work well with others? Are they comfortable collaborating with a team? 60% of hiring managers look for team-oriented candidates during the application process. Many companies succeed based on the work of groups and entire departments, not just individuals. So, as you review applications and conduct interviews, look for candidates with a history of collaboration and give and receive constructive group feedback.

6. Effective communicator: Understanding the benefits of clarity

Another top soft skill chosen by hiring managers was communication—56% looking for candidates' effective messaging. Ideal employees will understand the importance of good communication and how badly things can go wrong when a message is unclear or missed.

When looking for this quality among applicants, ask questions about their preferred methods of communication or for examples of good communication they've experienced. If their responses (verbal and nonverbal) align with your expectations, they may well become a great employee.

7. Flexible: Adapting in a meaningful way

Rounding out our list is flexibility, or adaptability, chosen by 51% of respondents. A good employee will not resist change blindly but instead embrace it and adapt to it as necessary for the business. Are the candidates you interview comfortable with unknown elements of a job? Are they willing to pick up new skills and adjust to shifting goals? If your applicants can demonstrate flexibility, you can be confident they'll adapt quickly to their new work environment.

You might not entirely agree with the importance of each soft skill, but you probably have an idea of what makes a good employee for your organization. One thing to keep in mind is that not every applicant will possess these research-backed qualities of a good employee—but some can be developed over time. Some candidates may not have much experience working in teams. Others may not have had to communicate with other departments, senior leaders, or external partners.

As we shift from a jobs market that favours employers to one that favours employees, don't let quality or quantity issues get you down. If you are confident in the skills and attributes you need in a candidate and have developed methods to locate them, you will already be one step ahead in the hunt for quality employees.

11 Traits of a Great Employer

This is NOT all one-way traffic. If you want to attract the best in the business, you'd better live up to THEIR expectations; this is a two-way interview, remember!

How do you measure up against the best of the best employers? The following are the TOP 11 reasons employees voted THEIR employer as the BEST PLACE TO WORK IN THE WORLD! The data is taken from over 17,000 respondents, listed in the order of priority to which they saw it as a BIG WIN.

1. You offer a flexible work schedule

In this era, employees expect to work where and even when they want. The 9-to-5 age is dead. By offering flexitime, allowing people to make schedules that work for them, and supporting those choices is an easy and affordable way to attract great employees.

2. You make your workplace Family/Pet-friendly

Aside from offering a laundry list of great benefits like unlimited sick days and health/dental/optician and therapy care, the top companies in the world also provide their employees discount childcare and day camp in the summer. So again, making a workplace kid-friendly or even pet-friendly is an easy, affordable, and welcome way to make your staff happy and WANT to be there!

3. You foster a culture that is creative and fun

What do you notice about the workplaces when you read or see profiles of high-flying, successful start-ups like Google or Facebook? For sure, they cultivate an

atmosphere of looseness and creativity. For example, items like ping-pong and Foosball tables tend to be liberally spread around. At Facebook, people go from meeting to meeting on scooters.

Adding an Xbox to the break room or simply a monthly games night is a simple way for small businesses to emulate these ideas quickly.

4. You cultivate the whole person

Great workplaces appreciate that people have various skills and interests. They are about more than having that person do their job every day. Great employers use that instead of denying that people have interests outside of work.

At some of the top businesses globally, employee benefits include "baseball games, surfing lessons, kayaking tours, white-water rafting, bonfires, bowling, and volunteering opportunities."

5. You don't tolerate idiots

We have all worked with idiots. Most of us have worked for an idiot or two. But the best companies in the world recognise the demonstrative environment one bad apple can have on the rest of the workforce, so if they have made a bad hire, it's about being big enough to recognise that and simply AIDING them off. YOUR bus!

6. You reward excellent customer service

That's not always financial, although it also might be. But you recognise and reward GREAT customer service. Both internally and externally.

7. You understand people have lives outside of work

So aside from flexible working, that's being flexible enough to recognise what matters. A school play or the local pantomime are important dates in a young child's life and should be treasured. Recognising this within the workplace is far more valuable than the early finish once every blue moon and likely to have far more impact when the head-hunters are on the prowl.

8. Your mission inspires your people to do their best

Great businesses are about a lot more than just making money, and the best employers get their employees to buy into their mission. Make it real, make it meaningful, and make it SO DAMN BIG that you need every ounce of effort from every single employee if you're ever likely to stand a chance of achieving it!

EXAMPLE

The mission of the pharmaceutical company Novo Nordisk is to "find a cure for diabetes." As one employee put it, "How many pharmaceutical companies can claim that their goal is to cure the very disease that keeps them in business?"

9. You listen

Make sure the door is always open. Your best employees are advocates for both you and your business. They are brimming with idea's suggestions for both the company and its employees. Being open to listening and responding to this goes a long way to BUY IN further.

Example: At CHG Healthcare, employee suggestions are not only welcomed but they are also actually implemented. As a result, the company now has an on-site fitness centre, daily fruit baskets, and a yearly wellness fair.

10. You have a good incentive program

Almost every company on the Fortune 100 list has a creative incentive program that rewards employees for a job well done. But, again, this doesn't HAVE to be financial. Read 5 Love Languages for employees to understand how a better understanding of how to communicate with people can go a long way in showing them you recognise and care for them and their contribution.

11. You pay a decent wage

People work for all sorts of reasons, but the primary one is salary. You cannot expect to be considered a great employer if you don't pay well. It need not be above the norm for your industry, just a good, honest, fair wage. If you don't, all the fancy creative benefits in the world won't make up for the fact that your people will feel underpaid and unappreciated.

Bottom line: Almost any of the benefits listed here can quickly and affordably be implemented by any small business, and all will make yours a better place to work.

How to Write a Job Posting:

Let's get to work here, with tips on creating a job advertisement that gets noticed on job boards or the busy free job posting sites.

1. Use a killer job title

This is an essential part of your job posting when posting to boards. When you write your title, include the name of the position and the top one to three things that will make the job attractive to an applicant.

2. Add an emotive introduction

This is a single paragraph that gives three to five details applicants will find most exciting about the job. It is like the lead that newspapers use to hook you into reading the full article.

3. Tell your company story

Information about your company that applicants want to know. How many years you've been in business, how long employees stay (if this shows that people stick with you), exciting clients or projects, equipment that applicants will be excited about, awards, accolades, and work culture facts that will interest them.

4. Really sell the position

Rather than the typical laundry list of bullet points, only include essential requirements for this job. Try to limit yourself to one to three things. Then provide information on work hours, pay, exciting co-workers, education opportunities, benefits or perks, and anything else applicants may find interesting.

5. Push your location

Moving is an obstacle to anyone considering your job that doesn't live in your region. If you want to attract people from other places, sell applicants on the location. Give them details about schools, activities, crime rates, things to do, etc. If your location is an easy commute from many key hiring areas, then spell out the actual commute time. A candidate will always be keen on a role that can cut their commute by 30 minutes.

6. Repeat why they should apply

This section is a quick bullet-pointed recap of the top five to six reasons someone should apply to your job. If you have a long job post, this will ensure that your key points are front-of-mind when the candidate is hovering over the apply button.

7. Spell out the application process

Detail everything from when they first apply to when they get hired. Candidates won't be left in the dark about "what happens next." This is especially important if you have a one interview hire role. Candidates who are available immediately will jump on roles like this as they can get a job in days vs weeks.

8. Have other people read it

Treat this job post writing exercise just as you would any other important piece of company marketing. Get multiple people to read it and provide you with honest feedback. Ensure you have fixed any errors before posting the job to hundreds of job boards.

9. Improve your email responses

Look at all the emails you send to candidates at each hiring process step. Pick them apart and ensure they are clear,

personal, and continue to sell the candidate on the role at every step. A poor first response to a candidate's application will undo all the excellent work you did in the job post getting them to apply.

Job Descriptions Are Not Job Posts:

Many people are confusing job postings with job descriptions. A job description should be a detailed, if somewhat dry, description of the responsibilities and expectations for a job that a company uses internally. A job posting is meant to sell applicants on your company, team, location, and all that make working for you great. So that's what you should be posting to job boards.

New Hire Checklist

New Hire Checklists for Employers for the First Year:

Day one:

1. Conduct a general job orientation with tour and introductions.

2. Review the first week's schedule and work hours.

3. Review professional ethics and code of conduct.

4. Review all policies, such as safety and security policies.

5. Explain the compensation and benefits.

6. Provide employee handbook and answer any questions.

7. Review position information.

8. Help set them up with computers or other equipment.

Week One:

1. Give employees any initial assignments.

2. Touch base each day to ensure they are settling in.

3. Review employee performance evaluations and set goals.

4. Review the employee's probationary period.

5. Check that equipment assigned to the employee is functioning and answer related questions.

6. Ensure the employee has met with key colleagues.

7. Invite the employee to connect with any company's social media accounts.

Month One:

1. Continue to provide regular feedback.

2. Ask for feedback from the employee.

3. Review past assignments.

4. Review upcoming assignments.

5. Ensure the employee is on schedule with training.

6. Check that employee payroll is running smoothly.

7. Schedule regular meetings to keep the employee engaged.

After Three Months:

1. Schedule an informal performance review.

2. Review past and future assignments.

3. Set performance goals.

4. Give and ask for feedback.

5. Check employee progress on training.

6. Discuss the end of the probationary period.

After 6 Months:

1. Conduct a six-month performance review.

2. Review employee goals and progress so far.

3. Set goals and objectives for the next six months.

4. Check that employee has received all necessary training.

After 1 Year:

1. Conduct a yearly performance review.

2. Recognize their first year at the company.

3. Discuss goals, projects, and plans for the upcoming year.

4. Answer any questions and give/receive feedback.

5. Discuss compensation and raise policies.

You have an effective induction system?

The Society for Human Resource Management is the world's largest HR professional society. It describes an employee induction as the process "through which new employees learn and adapt to the norms and expectations of the organization to quickly reach maximum productivity." Some people also use the term "onboarding" to include the time between offering someone a job and his or her first day.

What Makes a Program Successful?

Effective inductions are timely, organized and engaging, and give a good first impression of a company. They inspire new starters, set out an organization's mission and vision   for them, and educate them about the company's history, culture, and values. They also teach

them the technical skills they need and provide them with valuable information such as "who's who" in the business.

If done well, the induction process will allow a new starter to lay the foundations for important relationships within his team and across the wider organization and give him the best possible start in the organization.

Conversely, a poor induction program is either too full-on or not thought through properly. The most frequent complaints new starters make is that they're overwhelmed, bored, or left to "sink or swim." This can leave them feeling confused and make them less productive. If a new starter becomes disengaged, it may be very difficult to re-engage her. She'll soon leave, and you'll have to begin the recruitment process again.

Why Inductions Matter

The recruitment process can be time consuming and costly, so you want new joiners to contribute to the business as soon as possible. In fast-growth businesses, this can critically affect whether the business meets its potential or not.

An effective induction program – or the lack of one – can make the difference between a new employee successfully integrating and leaving very quickly. Research shows that this can affect engagement, staff turnover and absenteeism levels, and the employer brand.

When a candidate accepts a job, he may have to work several weeks' notice in his current role. It's therefore important that you, as his prospective manager, maintain contact with him and keep him engaged during this time. If you fail to do so, he could lose interest, change his mind, or – worse still – go to a competitor.

Top Tip: Inductions aren't just for new starters. Existing team members who have changed roles or are returning to work can also benefit from them.

A Best-Practice Guide to Successful Inductions

Don't leave your induction process to chance. Follow these steps, so that your new starter hits the ground running!

There are several important questions to ask when you are designing an induction program. These include:

1. How experienced is your new hire? It's important to tailor your approach depending on who you're inducting, so that the program is fit for purpose.
2. How formal do you want it to be? You may not need a rigid structure if your company is small, but it might be more efficient to run group sessions, for example, in a larger organization.
3. What first impression do you want to give?
4. What do new starters need to know about the work environment?
5. What policies and procedures should you show them?
6. How can you introduce new joiners to co-workers without overwhelming and intimidating them?
7. What do you need to provide them with (desk, work area, equipment, special instructions, and so on) so that they're ready to go from day one?
8. How can you make sure that the right people are available, so new team members feel informed and valued?
9. Where is your new starter based and what are her hours? If she works remotely or has different shift patterns to you, you'll want to coordinate schedules, at least for the first few days.

Ask for feedback from recent hires about their inductions and integrate any useful suggestions into future programs.

8.8 Team Appraisals

You have an effective team appraisal system (and everyone is working on 90-day development plans?

As jobs become more intricate, organizations must rely on teams of people to accomplish tasks. To evaluate job performance by teams of people, organizations institute team performance appraisals. Team performance appraisals assess the performance of teamwork on organizational performance. Team performance appraisals can range from recognition of individual performance and its contribution to group outcomes to only an assessment of the organization's performance. When only an organization's performance is evaluated, no individual appraisals are completed, and individuals do not receive performance ratings.

Types of Team Performance Appraisals

The culture and organizational structure of the workplace environment influence the type of team performance appraisal best suited to evaluate and measure performance. If work teams exist in the organization, but are used only occasionally to accomplish projects, individual performance measurements are used to determine a final rating of the employee. When an organization uses teamwork more frequently, performance appraisals still emphasize individual performance but introduce an assessment of the worker's contribution to the team effort. If an

organization uses a significant amount of teamwork to accomplish its objectives, team performance appraisals link team productivity measurements with individual performance measurements. Organization's with only a team approach do not utilize individual performance appraisals. Team performance measurements determine monetary rewards.

Elements of Individual Performance Appraisals

Individual performance appraisals are the traditional appraisals that measure individual performance against measurable objectives. Individual performance appraisals provide an opportunity for employees and supervisors to share ideas and reach mutually agreed upon objectives. Individual performance appraisals focus on the skills required to perform the current job and skills that must be acquired for promotion. Individual performance evaluations are tools to determine monetary compensation. This type of performance appraisal provides feedback and recognition to the individual.

Comparison of Individual and Team Performance Appraisals

Individual performance appraisals measure an employee's work against standard performance measures. Standard performance measures are derived from individual job descriptions. Often, a direct link exists between performance and pay based on an employee's job rating from the appraisal. Team performance appraisals assess an individual's contribution to the team.

Team performance appraisals are appropriate to support an organization's efforts to transition from an individual-based organization to a team-based organization. Team performance appraisal, for example, assess whether the team met its goals, produced a quality product, and worked well together.

8.9 Staying in the Loop

You get weekly updates from key team members?

Whilst we have already spent time looking at the benefits of dashboard across the business. To monitor, record and enable analysis of performance. This should never be at the expense of regular meetings with your key members of staff.

A dashboard doesn't portray emotion, it doesn't share concerns, or observations or the 'mood' of the business. And so, regular scheduled meetings to determine how well-oiled the machine is, and its impact is crucial as we continue to SCALE.

These meetings really ought to be diarised as the same time each week and have an agenda which includes AOB. The frequency, timeframe and content will soon be determined by the individuals concerned and enable you to keep a measure of the pulse within the business and be able to better determine where more time, effort, or consideration needs to be placed.

8.10 Future Org. Chart

You have an organisational development plan for:

1-2 Years? - 3-5 Years?

We've already determined the need for an organisational structure chart, and that it ought to be placed where it is visible to employee's and referenced regularly. However, as we push towards longer, more ambitious goals, so the FUTURE organisational chart must reflect this also.

8.11 5 Key Employee's

You have your 5 key business growth members in place:

Accountant (Tax Advisor)

An accountant performs essential financial functions related to the collection, accuracy, recording, analysis and presentation of a business, organization, or company's financial operations. In a smaller business, an accountant's role may consist of financial data collection, entry and report generation and may extend to both Payroll and reviewing 'other' key numbers within the business, such as pricing, profitability, and marketing activity in terms of PPC and Ad spend.

Marketing / Sales Manager

A marketing Manager oversees all marketing for the company and activities within the marketing department. Developing the marketing strategy for the company in line with company objectives. Co-ordinating marketing campaigns with sales activities. Planning and implementing promotional campaigns. Gathers results and works with both Sales and Accounts to ensure this is done cost effectively.

The objective of a sales manager is to meet company revenue targets through the activities of their sales representatives. Are responsible for motivating and advising their sales team to improve their performance, as well as hiring and training new sales representatives.

Solicitor/Lawyer

It is the role of a solicitor to the business legal advice and act on their behalf if necessary.

The general duties include work such as advising, drafting documents, research, negotiating, protecting the brand and good name of the business, and representing in court if required.

HR Manager

Human resource managers are responsible for ensuring that the overall administration, coordination, and evaluation of human resources plans, and programs are realized. Therefore, their responsibilities include Recruitment, induction, training & development, reviews, sickness, holiday, bonuses & entitlements, and disciplinary / dismissal proceedings if necessary.

Business Coach/Mentor

A business coach helps organizations to:

- Develop more effective strategies
- Make better 'people' decisions
- Increase organizational focus
- Strengthen company culture
- Increase individual and team accountability
- Better align the entire organization

What Makes a Good Business Coach/Mentor?

A good business coach/mentor doesn't tell leaders and team members how to get from point A to point B. They don't come up with a client's strategies or decide what's good and bad about company culture.

Instead, they work with clients to help them discover those things on their own.

A good business coach always does two things:

1. Coaches to the strengths and weaknesses of the company and its operations.
2. Coaches to help management uncover and resolve issues.

Coaching to Strengths and Weaknesses

Business coaching is all about working with management teams through a process of discovering strengths and weaknesses in relation to how the company operates. It is also a process of discovering the strengths and weaknesses of the company.

Once those strengths and weaknesses are revealed, we can begin working together to use both to the advantage of the company. As a business coach, I help facilitate to determine the goals of both the business AND the business owner. And Help, Support, Guide and Hold to Account both businesses and business owners to achieve those.

In terms of strengths, I help management teams discover how to maximize them across the board. I help them figure out ways to make sure those strengths are aligned toward reaching the company's goals. As far as weaknesses go, my job is to help leaders figure out how to identify and address them so that they can be either eliminated or minimized.

Coaching to strengths and weaknesses helps businesses understand where they are now and where they are headed in the future. This gives leaders an opportunity to set a new direction for the future, if need be, or realign the company to a future they have always known is there but have failed to pursue.

Coaching to Resolve Issues

Another thing a good business coach does, is help management teams uncover and resolve issues. Let's face it, every business has those nagging issues that get in the way of progress. It's not enough to keep them hidden in the closet where they can't be seen. They must be brought out into the open and dealt with.

The business coach is all business when it comes to identifying issues in need of resolution. Again, the coach's job is not to pull those issues out of the closet and force management teams to look at them. Rather, the business coach finds ways to lead team members to the door, encourage them to open the door, and then help them deal with what they find inside.

All of this is done without bias. Why is this important? Because bias is often what prevents companies from recognizing and resolving troubling issues. Management teams have a natural tendency to see things a certain way, thereby limiting their ability to easily recognize some of the most deeply rooted issues that are preventing the company from moving forward. A good business coach helps by bringing that shift of view into play.

No business coach can resolve client issues. Resolution is up to company leaders and team members. However, coaches can help facilitate management teams to discover and honestly look at issues so they can be effectively resolved.

8.12 The role of GM

You have recruited a General Manager

A general manager, sometimes simply called a GM, has broad, overall responsibility for a business or a business unit within a larger organization. The role is particularly common in large global or multinational organizations where businesses are organized along product lines, customer groups, or geographies. The general manager typically serves as the top executive for the unit and is responsible for strategy, structure, budgets, people, financial outcomes, and scorecard metrics.

Duties & Responsibilities

A general manager's duties and responsibilities cover a lot of ground, but these are some of the most common. They must typically:

- Oversee daily operations of the business unit or organization.
- Ensure the creation and implementation of a strategy designed to grow the business.
- Coordinate the development of key performance goals for functions and direct reports.
- Provide direct management of key functional managers and executives in the business unit.
- Ensure the development of tactical programs to pursue targeted goals and objectives.
- Ensure the overall delivery and quality of the unit's offerings to customers.
- Engage in key or targeted customer activities.
- Oversee key hiring and talent development programs.
- Evaluate and decide upon key investments in equipment, infrastructure, and talent.
- Communicate strategy and results to the unit's employees.

- Report key results to corporate officers.
- Engage with corporate officers in broader organizational strategic planning.

An individual in a GM role is a generalist who is familiar with all areas of the business and can coordinate processes and operations across the organization. A general manager usually must speak the languages of finance and accounting, operations, sales, marketing, human resources, research and development, and engineering.

In larger organizations, individuals viewed as having general management potential often work in a series of assignments, rotating through the various functions and gradually growing their expertise and responsibilities over many years.

In larger organizations, the general manager reports to a corporate executive, often the chief executive officer or chief operations officer.

Salary

A GM's salary can vary greatly depending on location, experience, and employer.

Median Annual Salary: £52,000

Top 10% Annual Salary: £107,500

Bottom 10% Annual Salary: £26,000

Education, Training, & Certification

The prerequisites to becoming a general manager vary depending on the requirements of the business and may include a minimum level of education, experience, and certification.

Education: Given the broad base of expertise and knowledge required for success in the role, general managers often have advanced degrees with an emphasis on a Master's in Business Administration (MBA) degree.

Experience and training: General managers typically have deep industry experience, and if they don't come up through the larger organization, they most likely have long histories of working for one or more competitors within the same industry.

Certification: Some universities and other educational institutions offer certificate programs in general management. Employers don't usually require candidates to have these certifications, but they could give candidates a competitive advantage.

Skills & Competencies

To be successful in this role, you'll generally need the following skills and qualities:

- **Strategic planning skills:**
  GMs must ensure the development and implementation of a clear strategic plan for an organization or business unit.
- **Financial planning skills:**
  GMs are responsible for looking at the future of the business and making key investments and investment recommendations.
- **Interpersonal skills:**
  GMs must be able to support the development of a healthy internal culture that retains key employees and encourages their professional development.
- **Leadership skills:**
  GMs are responsible for leading entire business units or divisions of an organization.

Work Environment

The role of a general manager isn't an easy one. A GM is accountable to his or her boss or corporate group for all the activities of the business unit with an emphasis on financial results. While GMs have a great deal of autonomy in operating within their business unit, they typically must justify significant investments as well as changes in key strategies or personnel. They have all the challenges of running a business, plus the challenges of reporting to a corporate group that is most likely focused predominantly on financial outcomes.

Work Schedule

GMs generally work during business hours but depending on the employer and the demands of the job, they may work some long days, late nights, and weekends.

You have multiple teams independently generating income for the business

What War Can Teach You About Business

The battle for supremacy in war or in business begins with the battle for resources. Whoever controls the supply lines gains an edge that will allow them to outlast their opponent. In war, resources mean things like weaponry, soldiers, and supplies. In business, your resources are your investments and human capital.

Obviously, if you're better funded and staffed, you have a leg up on the competition. But don't be dissuaded if you're not financially backed. You can still triumph.

Strategy

Nothing embodies war like the classic board game chess. Players oppose one another from across the table with all their pieces exposed. Every move is out in the open, and the absence of luck makes chess a game of perfect information. The only thing a player - or, for our purposes, a general or CEO - keeps from the opponent is their interior strategy.

Before the game, they have researched, organized, and planned an attack that will devastate their foe. This strategy of the chess grandmaster is your business plan. Only you and those you trust are aware of your ultimate strategy.

Tactics

Where strategy is an overall plan conceived in the mind, tactics are precise manoeuvres that effectively implement that strategy. To continue with the chess analogy, tactics involve specific moves that trap an opposing player. In business, your tactics are your day-to-day activities that move your business strategy forward. Each step you take should contribute to that strategy.

The best steps, or tactics, will contribute to helping you achieve your strategy in more ways than one. This increases your efficiency, giving you increased time to implement your overall plan.

Victory and defeat

In war, a defeat is usually measured in depressing numbers like body counts and by the consensus of major world governments. Some wars have clear losers. Other wars, such as political unrest, are harder to define in terms of winners and losers.

Business is similar, but clear defeats are certainly evident. For instance, a company goes bankrupt or loses market share.

The potential for growth is unlimited. And though competition for customers may be fierce, there is sufficient space for plenty of success. So, keep at it.

Diplomacy

Even the brutality of war has "rules" that have been put forward by the international community. If a country breaches these rules, it is made into an outcast. Likewise, entrepreneurs should follow an ethical code that supersedes their drive to succeed.

Businesses, like corrupt countries, may get away with unethical behaviour initially, but ultimately, they will be exposed and shunned. Luckily, the most successful countries are Masters of Diplomacy and strive to prevent conflict. Follow suit with your business. Act responsibly, sustainably, and morally. Impressed customers will flock to your business and other companies will model themselves after yours.

The very best method of achieving this is to Divide and Conquer.

We all know of the analogy of Eggs in Baskets, and why we ensure we have multiple income streams to prevent volatility. And yet many growing businesses fail to do this internally as well as externally!

I've seen some huge businesses disappear overnight because Google or Facebook changed an algorithm on which their entire business relied! Or the 70% of business that never survive after a fire, or the 60% after a flood!

To ensure the legacy of a business, we MUST ensure we create mini businesses within the entire business, which work autonomously within the business, that if one element breaks, it has little to no detrimental effect on the other elements of the business.

I've seen businesses fail because all relied on a single key member of staff, who has either taken ill, or left. And other businesses so reliant on single piece of software to which they only subscribe to and don't own! Only for the software company to be bought out, with the new owners quickly stopping support for this software in favour of everyone converting to their own!

8.13 Time to Multiply

You have Off-site quarterly meetings with your key growth members

I'm a huge advocate for OFFSITE meetings. It automatically brings a different level of intensity, of importance and removes distraction of day-to-day business.

It was Einstein who is reported to have said

> *"You will never overcome a problem,*
> *using the same level of thinking*
> *as that which created it"*

And an environment can be SO influential in our level and ability to think!

Professionals and executives employed by medium to large companies will inevitably attend all-day offsite meetings at some point. An offsite meeting brings your team together someplace apart from your usual office to hold a meeting, coordinate a strategy, or deliver training.

A meeting in this format will incur extra expense and will mean a day spent away from other essential daily tasks. Is it worth it?

10 reasons to organise an offsite meeting:

1. **Provide a morale boost**
   Most offsites are not just about getting the work out. They often include some sort of fun and entertaining team building exercise. The fun aspect of many offsite meetings can give help team members to feel good about their work. A new location can be exciting, especially in a hip, urban setting that can also be great for after-work happy hours.

2. **Give a new perspective**
   A change in physical environment can make an enormous difference when brainstorming new ideas. Meeting in the same office space at the same times can starve the brain of stimulation.

3. **Increase motivation**
   Business Matters magazine reminds us that an outside meeting has gravitas. People give it greater importance. It has a presence on their calendar, and so they think about it more, discuss it and plan it better.
   Offsite meetings can revitalize and reenergize employees. Due to the investment in their being invited, employees believe they are important and trust that their contribution matters. Because everyone has made a commitment to leave normal work behind for a day, they are more likely to fully engage with the topic of the meeting.

4. **Avoid interruptions**
   Far too much time is wasted by meeting attendees arriving late, checking their email, answering ad hoc requests for help, or a dozen other routine office interruptions? Avoid it all by taking them offsite, where they can focus better. The bottom line – much better productivity.

5. **Provide a challenge**
   Regardless of the activities planned or the problems to be brainstormed, just being in a new setting can be challenging. Breather, a Canadian company specializing in flexible office space, rightly says that challenged employees are interested employees.
   Disengagement will cost the company. Conversely, working together on strategic initiatives contributes to a shared feeling of success and improves overall company culture.

6. **Allow face-to-face networking**
   When it's critical to understand each other, nothing works like meeting in person. When a group shares the same physical space, you can pick up on non-verbal cues that would be missed over the phone or via video chat.
   Don't underestimate hand gestures, facial expressions, and body language – especially from team members who don't have the spotlight – and other nuances that allow colleagues to better relate to one another.

7. **Encourage camaraderie**
   Team building exercises are a key component of offsite meetings, and for good reason.
   Team members see each other in a different light and abilities emerge that may not be apparent in day-to-day office meetings. You are working with different skills. When you are really utilizing peoples' God-given talents, you find out different strengths and weakness than you do sitting at a desk. Plus, you are having a whole lot of fun doing it.

8. **Accomplish more on a time limit**
   Meeting in a different setting can emphasize the single-day timeframe, and this can encourage decision-making by imposing a deadline.

9. Team building

The best teams are bound together not just by a common goal, but also, by sharing a Significant Emotional Experience.

People pull together and form strong bonds after a natural disaster, or even after having worked overtime all night to meet a deadline. To build a team put them together and give them a task to do, or a problem to solve. You can include a team-building expert who can help you solve problems at the offsite. And you can give your team a significant emotional experience at the same time. They will bond and they'll solve problems better together.

10. Use the best technology

Using an offsite venue will give you access to different or newer technology. Business Matters says that specially designed meeting venues can also offer audio-visual experts along with the latest presentation tech at an affordable cost. This can help to show the company to its best advantage. It also works well when doing workshops or strategy meetings. Managers can focus on the content of the presentation, without worrying about technical glitches.

Conclusion

Not every meeting should be offsite, but there are numerous reasons to consider this option. A new venue gives your team a fresh approach to their work and to each other. It can be a memorable occasion where important skills are discovered, and bonds are made.

You have read: **Key person of influence** - *Daniel Priestley*

Many people think it takes decades of challenging work, academic qualifications, and a generous measure of good luck to become a Key Person of Influence. This book shows that there is a strategy for fast-tracking your way to the inner circle of the industry you love. Your ability to succeed depends on your ability to influence.

Good to Great - *Jim Collins*

To find the keys to greatness, Collins's 21-person research team read and coded 6,000 articles, generated more than 2,000 pages of interview transcripts and created 384 megabytes of computer data in a five-year project. The findings will surprise many readers and, quite frankly, upset others.

Built to Last – *Jim Collins*

The defining management study of the nineties showed how great companies triumph over time and how long-term sustained performance can be engineered into the DNA of an enterprise from the very beginning.

Conclusion

Whilst that draws an end to the final chapter in this book. It is but the opening chapter of what happens next.

I sincerely hope, that having got this far, all I have shared does nothing more than become another tragic case of *shelf development?*

I'd like to think, the information within these pages, have proven sufficient to inspire, motivate and enable you to think bigger, bolder, fast, further, and that you now see, by implementing all I have shared **will** make the biggest impact to both you, your business, and the impact it has on the world.

However, for some, there is still that uncertainty, trepidation, possibly even fear of applying all I've shared and the likely impact it may have?

Whether that's fear of failure, of 'getting it all wrong' and losing what you have already?

Or fear of success? Of achieving more than you have ever contemplated before, and the demands that may then put on you?

Or fear of the unknown? Of stepping out and doing something completely different, changing the status quo and taking the path less well trodden?

Whatever it is, there may well be a sense of concern. That, having read all I've shared, it is now time to **implement** this into **your** business.

And that niggling voice deep inside you that continually asks *"What if….."*

Well, I've got some **great news…**

Visit: **https://www.addazero.co.uk/free-scale-audit/** where you can access the #ADDAZERO Scaleup Scorecard.

30 NPS style (On a scale of 1-10) questions, based on the teachings from #ADDAZERO to determine the current scalability / vulnerabilities within your business.

Taking less than 10mins to complete, you can have an up to the minute, highly detailed and bespoke #ADDAZERO scaleup report clearly identifying the 'highs and lows' within your business, with practical guidance and advice on where to start your #ADDAZERO journey.

It shall also invite you to book a 'Scaleup Scorecard Review' with one of our highly qualified Scaleup Sherpa's during which we'll ensure every question you may have about the survey get's answered.

And, should you want some help in implementing this into your business, we can determine which of our #ADDAZERO Coaching/Mentoring/Consultancy programmes is best suited to you and your desired outcomes.

Visit: **https://www.addazero.co.uk/free-scale-audit/** to access your #ADDAZERO Scaleup Scorecard.

About Jay

Thank you for taking this step to significant and sustainable growth for both you and your business. By doing so, you are already a step closer than all those who chose to pass this book by for something with a 'sexier' cover.

I'm Jay Allen. Initially trained in Sociology and Psychology (*with a particular interest in communication and human behaviour*) and then transferred to Emergency Medical Science to join the British Army as a Rapid Deployment Advanced Trauma Medic.

Throughout my 12+ years of service, be than on operational commitments or field exercises worldwide, I never gave up my interest in observing communication and human behaviour. Despite my career coming to an unforeseen and rather abrupt end - medically discharged – diagnosed with Post Traumatic Stress Disorder (2000).

I have subsequently used my education, qualifications, knowledge and experience to work at the most senior level for two of the largest high street stores and regionally within change management for the NHS.

I branched out to become a business owner in 2005, and since then, have either bought, acquired or set up from scratch four of my own businesses, successfully exiting twice.

Besides a love of research, I now busy myself speaking to business leaders worldwide on the **#ADDAZERO** Methodology and as the founder of My TrueNORTH – The UK's Leading Ethical Business Coaching Company.

Through this, we have made it our mission to help and support 1,000,000 Business Owners to significantly and sustainably grow both them and their businesses, with the ultimate aim to **#ADDAZERO** to their personal disposable income.

For further details about **#ADDAZERO**, to sign up to our newsletter, and the **#ADDAZERO** podcast, Simply visit:

www.addazero.co.uk

Or, send an email to:

Iwantto@addazero.co.uk

Connect with me on:

LinkedIn:
https://www.linkedin.com/in/jayallenmytruenorth/

Opportunity

We've made it our mission, to support 1,000,000 Business Owners to #ADDAZERO to their Personal Disposable Income. That each business grows sufficiently to create at least 3 new roles, which in turn will enable us to eradicate unemployment, by generating sufficient work for more people than there are those actively seeking employment!

But we can't do this alone...

We invite suitably qualified and business experienced Coaches, Mentors, Trainers. As well as consultants and in-house Business Development Managers to enquire as to how to become a Licenced #ADDAZERO Practitioner

We'll provide all the training, training materials, mentoring and ongoing help and support to those with a desire to support others to #ADDAZERO to their Personal Disposable Income.

For further details, visit:
https://www.addazero.co.uk/aaz-coach-enquiry/

Printed in Great Britain
by Amazon

10196370R00153